HOLD FAST

HOLD FAST

Tasting God's Goodness in Deep Sorrow

CAMERON MALPASS

ISBN-13: 9781548681241
ISBN-10: 1548681245

In memory of my mom,
who taught me how to live and taught me how to die

TABLE OF CONTENTS

Let us hold fast the confession of our hope without wavering, for He who promised is faithful.

—HEBREWS 10:23

1

THE CALM BEFORE THE STORM

DAY AFTER DAY, for fourteen years in full-time service with the college ministry Cru, I gave to others with little concern or care for myself, and I teetered on the edge of burnout. Weary, spent, and ready to throw in the towel, I needed a break. My soul needed rest. Finally, I gave in and scheduled a much overdue sabbatical—a time to rest, recoup, and do what brings life to my soul. I could hardly wait.

Full of anticipation and determined to pack in as much activity as possible, I looked forward to reading books, tackling house projects, visiting the beach, and hosting friends. I also dreamed of planning a family vacation that was limited to my immediate family, since we rarely went away with just the seven of us. Before long, my plans exceeded my time off. I longed for time to sit with the Lord, to renew my spirit, and to grow deeper in intimacy with Him. September 29th couldn't get here quickly enough.

My sabbatical plan started with a trip to Tampa and Clearwater Beach, Florida, places dear to my heart after years of summer mission trips there with college students. Then I planned to spend the following ten days at home in Raleigh and wrap up with a trip to North Myrtle

Beach with a friend to finish out my time off. Hoping for that time with my family, I asked each of them to consider taking a long weekend to join me for my final days at North Myrtle. An obsessively scheduled person, I had my plan for how to use the time off all mapped out—or so I thought.

Three days into my sabbatical, while visiting my parents before my trip to Tampa, an old back injury flared up and left me flat on my back. Ice packs and Percocet became my new best friends. Excruciating pain coursed through my body from my neck to my toes, and I needed help from my mom to do the most basic tasks: rolling over, crawling out of bed, getting dressed, and even going to the bathroom. My initial back injury, years earlier, required months of recovery, so by day four of my sabbatical, my plans for the coming weeks began to drastically change. The trip to Florida or making it back to Raleigh to work on house projects now proved impossible. Instead, I was forced to face the fact that I would spend most, if not all, of my sabbatical in Goldsboro at my parents' house, lying flat on my back.

None of this resembled my well-laid plans…at all. I stared at the ceiling and asked the Lord, "Why now? What in the world are you thinking? Why would you allow this to happen? I needed this time off!" Bitterness and anger quickly took root in my frustrated heart.

God quickly reminded me of two very familiar passages in Scripture:

For my thoughts are not your thoughts, neither are your ways my ways, declares the Lord. For as the heavens are higher than the earth, so are my ways higher than your ways and my thoughts than your thoughts. (Isa. 55:8–9)

Be still, and know that I am God. (Ps. 46:10)

Taking the time to stop, to be still before the Lord, and to acknowledge Him and who He is don't really suit my "doer" personality. I am much more of a "doer" than a "be-er." Suddenly, I found myself forced to be still. Very, very still.

Through almost two decades of walking with Jesus, I had filled nearly thirty-two journals. In some seasons of my life, I was more faithful to journaling, and in other seasons, I left huge gaps in my writings. Yet these journals hold a window to my soul, a link to my past, and a beautiful picture of God's faithfulness over the years.

With the inability to travel, I decided to read back through these collections of my history, to take time to reflect back on two decades of transformation, and to linger in those places where Jesus had changed my life so much. It didn't take me long at all for my disposition to change from anger and bitterness to gratefulness for this special time of forced stillness.

This peek back into my early days as I began to walk with God brought back a glimpse of the beauty and goodness of those initial days of following Jesus, important months and years that had long been forgotten. As I read back through the pages of my life, God reminded me of His goodness and faithfulness to me. I saw countless prayers prayed and answered—many I of which I had completely forgotten about altogether. What a joy to read back through, to see these answered prayers, and to take the time to give God the glory for what He had done, even the things He had done that I had failed to recognize in the moment! He reminded me how He grew me up and matured me over the years and how my perspective and desires had changed with time. He reminded me of the times when He had pursued me and loved me. As tears flowed freely down my face, He reminded me of His faithfulness even in those times when, through my active disobedience, I chose anything but faithfulness to Him. He reminded me of an earlier time in my life when I experienced a sweetness, a nearness, and an intimacy with the Lord along with a passion and zeal for God's Word. This nearness, intimacy, passion, and zeal all described something noticeably absent in my current circumstances but something I longed to recapture.

Perhaps most importantly, He reminded me of His character as I thumbed through twenty years of scribbles on journal pages, recounting the many ways that God had revealed different aspects of His character to me. On October 8, 2014, after reading through all of these journals, I made a list of things I knew to be true about God's character. Here is that list as I wrote it in my journal that day:

Kind	Rock	Friend	God who hears
Faithful	Truth	Satisfier	God who understands
Holy	Gracious	King	Pursuer
Pure	Merciful	Lamb	Sanctifier
Just	Patient	Lion	Healer
Jealous	Good	Shepherd	Great Physician
Warrior	Beginning/End	Redeemer	Great I Am
Protector	Near	Lover of my soul	Most Beautiful
Provider	Sympathizes	Comforter	Most Valuable
Sovereign	Caring	True Joy	All-Present
In control	Careful	Trustworthy	All-Powerful
Worthy	Savior	Praiseworthy	All-Knowing
Constant	Father	Strong	Binds up wounds of the brokenhearted
Only True God	Maker	God who saves	Love
Defender	Creator	God who sees	Brings beauty from ashes

The second week in October, I penned these words describing the truths of God's character and had absolutely no idea how often I would begin to relearn these truths in the months and years to come. I could not have known then what I know now. But God knew. He saw. He cared. He went before me and prepared me for what was coming. Let's be honest: if I had gone to Tampa and Clearwater Beach or back to Raleigh to tackle numerous projects in my house those first few weeks in October, I would never have taken the time to truly be still and know that He is God!

Three weeks into my sabbatical and determined to get to the beach, I graduated from lying flat and staring at the ceiling to moving around slowly and deliberately. My best friend, Nicole, drove us to North Myrtle while I lay back in the passenger seat surrounded by ice packs (with extras on reserve in the cooler). Nicole stayed for the first half of the week, and my family joined me for the second half.

Though painful, riding to the beach and entering the land of salt air and sand between my toes proved medicine for my soul. Nicole and I had a wonderful first half of the week together. I enjoyed time on the beach reading a book called *Replenish*. Through his words, the author, Lance Witt, challenged me to slow down and rest—not just for a season of sabbatical but as a daily rule. I realized that to stay in ministry for the long haul, I needed to heed this challenge. I needed to take the time to linger with the Lord and not have such a hurried spirit in life. I vowed to read this book annually as a reminder.

On Thursday, my parents joined me, and on Friday, my brother, sister-in-law, and their two girls arrived. We had a blast! My nieces, Anna and Molly, instantly became enthralled with the lazy river at the condo. The water was breathtakingly cold, since it was mid-October, and we all volunteered my brother, Bert, to take one for the team and get in the lazy river with the girls. They giggled and laughed, and I swear they would have stayed in that river for hours if we had let them. We sat on the beach soaking in the sun and making sand castles, taking walks, and dipping our toes in the edge of the surf. We ate out at fun restaurants and enjoyed being together. We watched the sun peek over the horizon and spread its light across the water early one morning and captured amazing photos of the process. We went outlet shopping—my nieces knew exactly what face to make and what to say to convince Nana and Granddaddy to buy them anything they wanted. The time together flew by, and the memories we made quickly became priceless treasures. Too soon, Sunday arrived, so we packed our bags and headed back to North Carolina, promising ourselves we would take another family vacation together soon.

Little did I know at the time how much that family vacation would come to mean to me and how important it was that we laughed and played in that lazy river for those four days at a condo in North Myrtle Beach. Those particular days would mark the last time that our family would experience "normal".

2

THE C-WORD

I THINK I INHERITED my love for serving, my capacity to lead, and my ability to persevere from my mom. She modeled strength of character, fierce resolve, and unwavering positivity both in her job and, especially, in our family. Sacrificial, selfless, and generous, she made her life an anthem dedicated to doing for others. I am hard pressed to think of a time when she complained or needed much for herself. Her unmatched "push through it" mentality allowed her to perform at a high capacity, juggle multiple things at one time, and essentially serve as everyone's go-to person for any task or problem that needed solving.

Just days after returning from our sweet family vacation at the beach, my mom came home early from work complaining of stomach pains. Over her thirty-five years as the business administrator at Wayne Country Day School, my mom rarely took time off from work, except to spend time with her family. I can't remember a time when she missed work for being sick, so I knew something must really have been wrong.

For about a week, she and her doctor went back and forth with possibilities to explain her constant pain. Could it be constipation? Diverticulitis? Some virus? Or possibly something worse? She described the pain as similar to that of childbirth, yet unrelenting and without breaks between the contractions. After a week of this labor-like pain, she told her doctor she wanted a scan done because she just knew that something was wrong.

My sabbatical ended with our family beach trip, and my reentry to the ministry world took me to the mountains for a conference for ministry directors. During a meeting break, I noticed a missed call from my mom and stepped out of our crowded meeting room into a dark and empty adjacent meeting room to return the call. She told me very matter-of-factly that she had gotten the CT scan that morning and that her medical doctor had called her late in the day to report a "suspicious mass" on the scan. He referred her to her gynecologist for an appointment the next day. I felt the breath knocked out of me as if someone had punched me in the gut. How could this be happening? I quickly talked myself off the cliff—maybe it was nothing. Maybe it was just a benign cyst that needed to be removed. I certainly didn't need to overreact, did I? I had another hour and a half of meetings to sit through, so I needed to pull myself together. I longed to stay in the dark, empty room and pretend like reality didn't exist on the other side of the heavy meeting room door. But reality did exist, and I needed to face it. I walked out of that room a changed person, gripped with a mix of anxiety and fear and a sudden lack of care or concern for anything that had seemed important in my meeting just minutes before.

The conference ended the next day, and with remnants of my back pain still present, I rode in the passenger seat while my coworker and friend, Daniel, drove my car the four hours back to Raleigh. About half-way through the trip, my phone rang with my mom on the other end of the call. I hesitated, simultaneously desiring to hear what the doctor had said and also desiring to escape from reality and pretend that no such doctor's appointment ever existed. When I reluctantly answered, she shared that the appointment had not lasted long at all because upon one look at her scan, he told her that she needed to see a specialist, someone with more experience than he had. He referred her to a gynecological oncologist at the University of North Carolina Cancer Center who was willing to see her the next day.

So there it was: the C-Word. It hung in the silent spaces of our phone call, where words seemed woefully inadequate. The word "cancer" brought an instant fear, a sudden shock, and it stole our breath away. I always thought that cancer happened to other people, but not to us. "So did he say you for sure have cancer?" I uttered.

My mom went on to explain that he didn't necessarily say that, but that was most likely why he was sending her to the experts at UNC. Fear continued to creep into my heart and crawl across my mind all the way back to Raleigh. You see, my mom was my person—the one who called me every day and the one who, on any given day, knew what I was doing and, more importantly, how I was doing. She was the one I, for years, had feared losing the most. She was the one without whom I couldn't imagine living through a single day. And now she might have cancer. Pretending I would wait to worry until we knew more specifics, I told Daniel that I was fine. I was wearing a mask and saying what I felt like I was supposed to say, while on the inside, fear and all of the "what ifs" quickly took over. In horror, my mind began to run through all of the possibilities that lay before my mom. That night (and honestly, for many nights following), I wept. I cried out to the Lord in desperation, "Please, Lord, not my mom."

The next day brought many emotions for my mom and dad as they made the two-hour drive from Goldsboro to Chapel Hill, NC. They found their way to the string of hospitals on Manning Drive, parked in the parking deck, and searched anxiously for the correct hospital to enter. They met with multiple oncologists that day and came up with a plan to surgically remove the grapefruit-sized tumor taking up residence in my mom's abdomen. But first she had to endure more tests to determine where the tumor connected itself. The oncologists wanted all of the right players in the operating room for surgery, so they scheduled a colonoscopy and other tests to see exactly which organs might be affected by this tumor. That meant more waiting, more pain. My mom still felt pains similar to childbirth, and the fast-growing tumor inside of her mockingly showed itself through her skin as her belly continued to swell, almost as if these labor-like pains might actually produce a child.

As my mom and dad left the oncology center, they decided to go get some lunch before heading back to Goldsboro. With directions from regulars at the hospital, they walked from the women's hospital next door to the children's hospital to find the cafeteria. As they neared the children's hospital, they noticed a parade of tiny patients, dressed up in Halloween costumes and trick-or-treating through the halls of the hospital. Getting closer to the crowd, my parents saw that these bald-headed children, most likely fighting cancer, displayed their costumes with pride and brandished their IV poles with courage. My parents stood on the sidelines that day looking in at a world that they knew nothing about and, with tears streaming down their faces, caught glimpses of a journey that our family could not possibly begin to fathom. That night, my mom called Bert and told him to hug his girls a little tighter and to enjoy every minute of walking through their neighborhood trick-or-treating. You never know when the privilege might be taken away without notice.

When I heard from my parents that night and realized more deeply the battle we faced, I decided that it was time to call on friends to join with me in the battle. I believe in prayer, and I believe in the need for community and people coming together during hard times. So I sent out my first of many emails to a group of trusted friends begging and pleading with them to get down on their knees, along with me, and ask God to somehow be near in the scary days and weeks ahead.

As I sent the initial email requesting prayer, my mind drifted back to just weeks earlier when I deemed my sabbatical ruined because my plans had changed. Now I knew that my sabbatical had not been ruined at all. Instead, the Lord had forced me to be still and had given me the fuel that I needed to face what could be some of the hardest days of my life. I stopped that night to praise God for reminding me of His true and constant character, even when things around me seem uncertain and scary. God reminded me that night of Psalm 46, which says:

God is our refuge and strength, a very present help in trouble. Therefore we will not fear though the earth gives way, though the mountains be moved into the heart of the sea, though its waters roar and foam, though the mountains tremble at its swelling. (Ps. 46:1–3)

He is my refuge and my strength and I don't have to fear when the earth gives way. I thought to myself, "Yes, Lord, this is what I needed to hear." In so many ways, it felt like the earth was giving way and the ground beneath me was shaking and slipping out from under me. But He is my refuge and strength. He is the constant One when nothing else in life seems constant and sure.

I had actually spoken on this topic of God's immutability to a group of college students years before. The outline of my talk was quite simple: "People change. Circumstances change. But we can have a thankful heart because God never changes." In my talk, I referenced the following Scriptures:

For I the Lord do not change. (Mal. 3:6)

Every good and perfect gift is from above, coming down from the Father of lights, with whom there is no variation or shadow due to change. (James 1:17)

Of old you laid the foundation of the earth and the heavens are the work of your hands. They will perish, but you will remain;

they will all wear out like a garment. You will change them like a robe, and they will pass away, but you are the same, and your years have no end. (Ps. 102:25–27)

Jesus Christ is the same yesterday and today and forever. (Heb. 13:8).

Rejoice always, pray without ceasing, *give thanks in all circumstances*; for this is the will of God in Christ Jesus for you. (1 Thess. 5:16–18)

Do not be anxious about anything, but in everything by prayer and supplication *with thanksgiving* let your requests be made known to God. (Phil. 4:6)

People change. Circumstances change. But thankfully, God never changes. Years ago, when all seemed well in my life, speaking on this outline proved easy. It became a bit harder to cling to these truths when I felt my life turning upside down and spinning out of control. As I pondered this talk that I had given, I thought about the reality that hundreds of staff members and students involved in Cru would now watch my responses as I weathered this impending storm. That night, I wrote down a simple prayer in my journal:

Lord, if this is cancer, would you give each of us the grace to walk through this and continue still to praise you, continue still to trust you, and continue still to believe in your character? Jesus, I pray that as staff and students watch me walk through this, they would say, "How great is Jesus!"

3

HOLD FAST

THE INITIAL SURGERY went as planned. My dad, Bert, Nicole, and I waited for about three hours in the surgical waiting room that day. After completing the surgery, my mom's oncologist talked to us in the hallway outside the waiting room. With confidence, he shared that he was able to remove all of the now bowling-ball-sized tumor that he could see. My mom made it through the surgery fine, although they did have to cut out part of her small bowel and reattach it, which would make her recovery more involved. We saw her in recovery, and soon after, a transport guy rolled her back to her room on the sixth floor, the gynecological oncology wing. Bert and I worked out a schedule and began to switch off spending nights with her, and my dad joined us during the day.

So began my relationship with the sixth floor. I didn't expect for it to begin to feel like a home away from home, but somehow it did. It is strange how a place like an oncology ward, where you would never wish to be, could become a place of comfort and refuge. I had no idea that over the course of the next year, I would become friends with the nurses and CNAs on the floor. I had no idea that it would become second nature to get up and walk to the family pantry on the floor to get something to drink or eat. I had no idea that the vinyl pullout chair would become a place that I would so often lay my head during the upcoming weeks and months. But it did, and I quickly became grateful for that place.

In times like these, I learned to find joy in and celebrate the little things. I found joy in being in Chapel Hill, on the campus of my alma mater. I found joy in the Tar-Heel-blue footprints that graced the walls in my mom's hospital room. I found joy in seeing UNC written on every piece of paper, coffee cup, and supply brought into my mom's room. I found joy in watching the homecoming football game on the Jumbotron at Kenan Stadium outside of my mom's hospital room window. And I found joy in watching my diehard, NCSU-loyal brother and dad have to sit among such beauty! One day, surrounded by all things Carolina blue, my dad said, "You know, for all of my life I have loathed this place. But honestly, right now, there is no place I would rather be."

For all of us, the sixth floor provided such comfort. Surrounded by some of the top oncologists and cancer researchers in the country, gratitude arose as we continued to taste God's goodness in putting us so close to such great physicians and cancer care.

Day one after surgery, I quickly learned that sleep is next to impossible in a hospital with round-the-clock people coming in to check blood levels, IVs, and every other possible thing that might need checking at 3:00 a.m. Sleeping late also never happens. Doctors' rounds started around 6:00 a.m. Every morning, a team of doctors on my mom's case would come in bright and early to see us and talk with us. The morning after her surgery, her team came in and shared with us that the preliminary pathology reports showed the tumor as "bad cancer" and that more extensive pathology reports would identify the specific kind and stage. That morning, we talked about how, though it appeared they got it all, the possibility of microscopic malignancies left behind still existed, and those possibilities would call for aggressive chemotherapy.

While simultaneously overwhelmed and sad, a strength and fight began to well up inside of us—a fight that we knew without a doubt would lead us down a long and exhausting road.

For days, my mom could not eat or drink anything. She looked miserable with a tube coming out of her nose, clearing the contents from her stomach. A slow process began as we got her up out of the bed. Arm in arm, little by little, she and I took steps building up to what would become our "walks around the block." The sixth floor lay in the shape of a rectangle, and so we built up to walking around the whole rectangular hall. Within days, we walked multiple trips around the block, greeting and encouraging other recovering patients along the way. Mom gained strength as the fight inside of her grew with each step she powered through. As she gained strength, I felt exhaustion beginning to take over my body, but I knew that the road ahead was long and that there was no time for exhaustion, so I pushed through as well, cherishing the time I had with my mom and grateful for the every-other-night breaks to go home, shower, and sleep.

My mom, a fighter, continued to gain strength, and with fierce determination, she did everything the nurses and doctors asked her to try to do. After a week in the hospital, they released her to go home and rest and recover for a few weeks before returning to meet with the oncologist to set up chemo plans. Our main goals were for her to gain strength and gain weight at home. She had lost twenty-three pounds since the whole ordeal had started.

A friend of ours who had faced his own bout with cancer told us that this journey would feel like a roller coaster, with ups and downs and twists and turns, often when least expected. I am not a big fan of roller coasters. Like I mentioned earlier, I am a planner. I like to know what to expect. I like control. So while the roller coaster analogy could not have been more spot on, I didn't care for it one bit. I dreaded the ride and, quite frankly, wanted to leave the amusement park. If only it worked like that with cancer. If only you could choose to leave the amusement park.

On December 5th, my dad and I took my mom back up to Chapel Hill. Mom had some good days but also had a lot of not-so-good days. Adjusting to her many new medications had been hard for her. Adjusting to a new digestive system that had been torn apart and reattached in the surgery caused all kinds of issues with her control of her bowels and ability to use the bathroom. She continued to struggle to eat, and the weight continued to fall off of her slender body.

So we sat in the oncologist's examination room, already battered and bruised and ready to get off of the ride, when in reality the ride was just beginning. Dr. Kim, the oncologist, told us that my mom had stage three ovarian carcinosarcoma, a very rare and fast-growing type of ovarian cancer with a high likelihood of reoccurrence. We talked through chemo options and made a plan for a chemo cocktail that would last all day and would cycle through every three weeks. This would continue for eighteen weeks for a total of six rounds.

Realizing that my mom would need round-the-clock care for at least the first week or two after chemo, I decided to call in reinforcements. My mom's family is large and extraordinarily close. On one side of her family, my mom has sixteen first cousins, several of whom function more like siblings. So I called on her "sister-cousins" for help and they sent me their schedules and times they could fly or drive to Goldsboro. I worked out a plan to mesh together all of our schedules, arranged flights and rides to and from the airport, and displayed all of these plans in a color-coded care calendar for the following five months of treatments. The schedule allowed me to be with my mom for most of her chemo treatments and the week following each treatment. Her sister-cousins filled in the second weeks and times when I could not be there.

Dr. Kim had warned us not to look things up on the Internet, but of course, I did. Ovarian cancer—the "silent killer," they call it. With symptoms often masked as everyday ailments, it is rarely caught at an early stage and is one of the most deadly cancers for women. Only 20 percent of women diagnosed with late-stage ovarian cancer are alive five years later. More specifically, ovarian carcinosarcoma is a cancer so rare that there's little data on it, leaving the survival rate merely eight to twenty-four months.

Eight months? I couldn't breathe. What if my mom was gone in eight months? How could something so deadly be living inside of her? Again, I wept. As I wept, I felt like I was suffocating until I heard a still, small whisper from the Lord as the following words came across my mind: "Do you trust me?"

Did I trust Him? I wanted to say, "Yes, of course I trust you," but what if He asked me to surrender my mom to Him? What if He asked me to say good-bye to her within the next eight months—would I trust Him then? I wrestled with the Lord. Could I honestly say that I trusted Him? My mind drifted back to my sabbatical—reminders of His faithfulness, His provision, His trustworthiness, and His character.

"Yes, Jesus, I trust you. Not my will, but your will be done."

These very familiar phrases were now clouded with fear as I hesitantly whispered them back to the Lord. As I placed my fear and my trust in His hands over the course of the next few weeks, I memorized the following two verses:

Fear not, for I am with you; be not dismayed, for I am your God; I will strengthen you, I will help you, I will uphold you with my righteous right hand. (Isa. 41:10)

But he said to me, "My grace is sufficient for you, for my power is made perfect in weakness." Therefore I will boast all the more gladly of my weaknesses, so that the power of Christ may rest upon me. (2 Cor. 12:9)

Mark, a dear friend and co-worker of mine, lost his father to cancer several months prior. He knew all too well the road we were walking. It was hard even to talk to Mark on the phone in those days, because the tears came quickly for us both. Having gone through this journey ahead of me, Mark was faithful to text me often with prayers and encouragement for the days. At the end of each of his texts, he would always write, "Hold fast."

At first, it didn't mean much to me. But the repetition of those words and the truth behind them began to sink into my heart and mind. Hold fast. What I needed more than anything was to cling to, or hold fast to, Jesus—the only constant in this storm. Hebrews 4:14 says, "Since then we have a great high priest who has passed through the heavens, Jesus, the Son of God, let us hold fast our confession." Hebrews 10:23 says, "Let us hold fast the confession of our hope without wavering, for he who promised is faithful." As Mark's reminders to hold fast continued in the weeks and months ahead, I clung to these truths. I prayed diligently that the Lord would help me to hold fast to hope and truth, even when the storms of life threatened to pry my hands from those very things.

One morning while processing with the Lord, God brought to my mind the verse in Job 38:11 where God draws the boundaries of the ocean and its waves. I knew that God was in control, and if He could control the exact place of the ocean's rolling waves, He could also control any bit of disease left in my mom. He could wipe it out. He could cause it to shrink or cause it to grow—because He is God and He is in control. He knows what is best and does all things for His glory.

At the same time, I was reading a book called *The Red Sea Rules*, and the chapter I was reading described God as more concerned with His glory than my relief. What an intriguing concept. When things in my life were going well, I doubt I would have pondered such a statement. I would have agreed wholeheartedly, "Of course He is more concerned with His glory than my relief." However, with my mom's life and death on the line, trusting that His glory is more important than my mom or her relief felt daunting. So my prayer in those days became, "Lord, help me to trust you enough to care more about your glory than my or my mom's relief."

4

THE STORM WITHIN A STORM

S ATURDAY MORNING, ONE week after our appointment with the oncologist and one week before my mom's first scheduled chemo treatment, I noticed that my dad was very sick. In recent years, he had struggled several times with pneumonia, and his symptoms led me to believe the pneumonia was rearing its ugly head again. I knew from experience that I needed to get him to the doctor fast to avoid a hospital stay. Agreeing to go to an urgent care clinic, my dad began to work his way to the car, but even that seemed unusually challenging for him. Once at the clinic, the doctor revealed to us that my dad had the flu, which seemed to be spreading like wildfire that year, unhindered by the vaccine that many had counted on for protection. My dad mentioned to me that several of his employees at our family business had been diagnosed with the flu earlier in the week. With Tamiflu in tow, we headed back home, and I enforced a strict plan to keep my dad quarantined from my mom. Her body could not handle cancer and the flu and the upcoming chemotherapy, where for hours her doctors would pump poison into her body to kill the cancer cells. I made a practice of wearing gloves any time I came near my dad, and I became a professional at washing my hands. Determined to care for both of my parents, my highest goal became keeping my mom, and myself, from contracting the flu.

Early Monday morning, discouragement set in as my mom began to show symptoms of the flu. With a few phone calls, her doctors called in a Tamiflu prescription and warned us that she needed to be fever free for twenty-four hours before she could receive the scheduled chemotherapy on Friday. My head was spinning. I continued to care for my parents and prayed fervently that I might be spared from this vicious attack on our house. Within an hour of getting the Tamiflu for my mom, the phone rang and my uncle, who lives an hour away, asked if we could go check on my grandparents, who lived seven doors down. He had received a strange phone call and thought that they might need some help. Stretched thin and overwhelmed by all that was going on in our house, I agreed to check on another house and see how I could help. Because of the strangeness of the call, my dad decided to go with me. Flu or no flu, these were his parents, and if something was wrong, he wanted to be there.

When we arrived, we found my grandfather had fallen and was barely breathing. Immediately, I called 911 and asked for help. I got down on the floor, placed a pillow under his crooked neck and assured him that help was on the way. From that point, things began to happen quickly. I ran to open the front door and welcomed the paramedics. While I filled out paperwork, my dad explained my grandfather's long history with asthma and breathing troubles. Meanwhile, the paramedics worked to get my grandfather immobilized on a spinal board and transferred to a stretcher. My dad and I followed the ambulance to the hospital while I frantically called my uncle and asked him to come to Goldsboro to help. At some point between the house and the hospital, my grandfather lost consciousness and stopped responding. An hour later, hooked to a ventilator that would take each breath for him, doctors told us to prepare for the worst.

Prepare for the worst? Seriously? The worst already happened when a rare and deadly cancer took up residence in my mom's body. The worst already happened when my mom and dad both got the flu the same week our cancer battle was to begin. And now an ER doctor is telling me to prepare for the worst? "Lord, are you there? Do you see what is happening? Can I trust you?"

Wrestling with God in my inner being once again, a verse I memorized long ago came to mind: "Rejoice always, pray without ceasing, give thanks in all circumstances; for this is the will of God in Christ Jesus for you" (1 Thess. 5:16–18). With each passing life event, trusting Him became harder and harder. Yet I knew this Scripture was true. Thankful for a foundation of faith and for times of thanking God in the now seemingly small trials of life, I felt prepared to thank Him in the bigger trials. And so with earthly fear and eternal faith warring within me, I chose a thankful heart. I thanked God for the trials we faced and prayed earnestly for Him to help us.

Moved to the intensive care unit and hooked up to more tubes and machines than I thought possible, my grandfather lay fighting for his life while my mom, less than a mile away, was at home fighting for hers. Meanwhile, I summoned strength that I did not know I had and began shuffling back and forth between two houses and the hospital. I was caring for my mom, my grandfather, and my grandmother, who needed round-the-clock care now that her primary caregiver, my grandfather, was not there.

The next day, doctors confirmed that my grandfather also had the flu, which now had affected every single one of the employees at our family business, where my grandfather had visited the previous week. He continued to lie lifeless in the ICU bed as his sisters, sons, and other grandchild, my brother, arrived at the hospital.

Sadness overwhelmed us with great reason, but my grandfather's faith brought us hope. He knew Jesus, so while deep sadness of the sudden impending loss filled our minds and faces during those days, an unexplainable peace also shone through. Knowing that my grandfather would never fully recover from the oxygen deprivation his brain had experienced, we trusted Jesus to take him Home in His timing, knowing that was best.

Meanwhile, we prayed that my mom's fever would break and that the Tamiflu would shorten the time that the flu wrecked her body. By Wednesday, the fever broke, and we celebrated. That same day, my grandmother and I both began to show flu symptoms, now the fourth and fifth members of our family to be diagnosed with the flu in less than a week's time. We both took Tamiflu. I imagine the local pharmacist felt sorry for our family by this point, especially a few days later when my uncle filled a prescription for himself as well.

By Thursday, my grandmother was too weak to stay at home, so we called 911, and an ambulance took my grandmother to the hospital. By Friday, feeling as if I had been run over by a truck while my grandmother and grandfather were separated by a few floors at the local hospital, my dad drove my mom to another hospital in Chapel Hill to begin her first chemotherapy treatment.

I was living a nightmare, and yet Jesus drew near. He provided for our family in those days. Without asking for help, friends and members of our church began to leave food and supplies we might need on the front porch. Again, in the midst of great sadness, sickness, and fear, I knew without a doubt that God sees. He knows. He cares for us deeply.

The day of my mom's first chemo treatment, I received a text message with a picture of a small note that I had written to a friend months earlier. My friend was living overseas, and I had sent her off for the year with notes to open on random dates throughout the year. The note that I had written for her to open on December 19th read. *"Christ is better! This is always truer than what you may be feeling. Cling to truth!"*

When I had written this note I had no idea how much I would need to receive it back in that exact moment. Again, I found myself tasting the goodness of God, who had me write something for a friend in August that I would desperately need to read myself in December.

With fear and uncertainty, my mom and dad entered the chemo infusion room at UNC that day with assumptions of what they thought they might experience. In general, we all assumed that the day would be unpleasant, surrounded by very sick people who would mirror what life held for my mom down the road of cancer treatments. My mom and dad described a very different scene when they returned to Goldsboro that night. My dad described the scene, which was not unpleasant at all, as the most peaceful his life had seemed in recent weeks, almost as if he and my mom had gotten away for a few hours on a deserted island. Shocked, I asked them to tell me more. They described the kind and caring chemo nurses, friendly patients, and a floor-to-ceiling window that overlooked a beautiful garden; the sun shone through and brought a warmth to the afternoon. Honestly, it sounded more like a day at the spa than the hell that we had been facing earlier in the week. The nurses told my mom that she would feel great on Saturday and would crash on Sunday. They warned us to gear up for a hard week to follow.

Coming out of my flu symptoms and beginning to feel somewhat normal, though still weak, I retook my place as caregiver, vigilantly tending to my mom and occasionally sneaking up to the hospital for brief visits with my grandparents. Saturday passed, and just as the nurses predicted, the steroids given to my mom during her chemo treatment gave her a strength, energy, and chattiness we had not seen in recent months. My dad and I laughed at the change and even wondered when and if my mom might stop talking. Seeing her act like herself again left us giddy.

But then Sunday came. As predicted, midmorning, her body crashed. Suddenly, all of her strength was gone, and I could see the shadows of sickness falling across her face. Sunday evening just before dinner, we asked a neighbor to sit with my mom while my dad and I made a quick trip together to the hospital. My grandfather's health had declined, if that was possible, and we sensed the time that he may leave this world drawing near. My dad and I left the hospital in silence that night, tears streaming down our faces. Once home, we prepared dinner, and though weak, my mom sat with us at the dinner table, determined for life to go on as usual.

Partway through the meal, I very suddenly noticed that my mom did not look well. She pushed her plate away, and I immediately jumped up to grab the pink bucket that we kept nearby in case the nausea that often accompanied chemo showed up. In one swift motion, I removed her plate from the table and shoved the pink bucket in its place. To our surprise, my mom stood up and walked carefully toward the kitchen sink. Perplexed, I thought that perhaps she preferred to puke in the kitchen sink than in the pink bucket, but as I watched her closely, I saw her hand and then her entire arm begin to slowly slip into the soapsuds-filled water. Quickly I yelled, "She is passing out," and my dad grabbed her from behind as I moved a chair over to the sink for him to sit her in. Her eyes opened and slightly rolled back in her head, and she did not respond to our calling her name or gently hitting her face. I grabbed the phone and, in the back of my mind, thought, "Is our family really about to call 911 for the third time this week?"

Fear pulsed through my heart and tears brimmed as I heard my dad say, "This cannot be happening."

Seconds that felt like minutes later, my mom regained consciousness and wondered how she had gotten from the table to a chair by the kitchen sink. Too weak to move from place to place on her own after that, my dad or I followed my mom cautiously, step for step, waiting to catch her if she passed out again.

Days later, released from the hospital, my grandmother returned home and another uncle, who had flown in from his home in England, stayed to help care for her. With my mom still regaining strength and my grandfather still in the hospital, we celebrated Christmas with less fanfare than usual. We welcomed a sweet simplicity to our usually busy and full holiday. We capped off the holiday with a "hat and scarf party," surprising my mom one night when my dad, brother, sister-in-law, nieces, and I walked into the living room all wearing different hats and scarves that we had bought knowing my mother would need them one day soon. We laughed and cried and made the most of the reality we faced.

Taken off of the ventilator and breathing on his own for a few days, my grandfather still took labored breaths and had little to no chance of a full recovery. On December 30th, with my uncle by his side and my dad on his way to the hospital, my grandfather breathed his last breath here on Earth. With deep sadness at the loss of the family's patriarch, we rejoiced that he no longer lived in a broken body and would never again struggle to breathe. I clung to the truth in John 11:25–26: "I am the resurrection and the life. Whoever believes in me, though he die, yet shall he live, and everyone who lives and believes in me shall never die." My grandfather believed and trusted in Jesus, which leaves no fear in death and no doubt for me that he lives on eternally outside of the world that my finite eyes can see.

While preparations were made for my grandfather's funeral, my mom began to notice clumps of her hair falling out. Determined to go to his funeral, even though my dad and I thought it best for her to stay home, my mom decided it was time to shave her head. She said matter-of-factly, "I don't want to hug someone at the funeral and leave a clump of hair on their shoulder."

So the day before my grandfather's funeral, my mom, my dad, Bert, and I gathered around her as my uncle shaved the remaining hair on her head. I had feared the trauma of shaving her head, when in fact the beauty of the event actually surprised me. Her strength and courage powerfully showed her inner beauty, and the glow in her face and pronounced blueness in her eyes drew my attention to her outer beauty. In that moment, I found my mom more beautiful than ever.

Years ago, a friend shared the following concept with me: it is better to gaze at Jesus and glance at my circumstances than to glance at Jesus and gaze at my circumstances. For years I have shared this with the students I disciple. And now I needed to preach it again to myself. Though everything about my circumstances screamed horror, pity, and tragedy, I knew I did not have to place my focus there. So I began to ask Jesus to help me place my ultimate gaze on Him. I knew that if I could truly grasp even a glimpse of His beauty, His goodness, and His character, things on Earth would pale in comparison. I prayed, asking the Lord to show me His beauty, to reveal to me His goodness, and to remind me of His character and faithfulness to me. Taking the focus off of my circumstances and placing that focus on the One who was worthy of my gaze brought life and hope into a situation that others might call hopeless. "Oh, taste and see that the Lord is good! Blessed is the man who takes refuge in Him!" (Ps. 34:8).

5

HE SEES

S TRIVING FOR NORMALCY in my life, I headed to my weekly Cru staff meeting one Friday morning with excitement about our staff women's lunch to follow. I also had great anticipation for a weekend at my house in Raleigh (the first in months) to clean, do laundry, and catch up on life. At the end of our staff meeting that morning, I got a call from my mom's sister-cousin Nancy, who had flown in from Florida and was on call as caregiver that week for my mom. She shared that she had taken my mom to Chapel Hill because she was passing some blood. They had done a scan and detected another mass, which could be any number of things: an abscess of fluid, a hematoma, or God forbid, more cancer. Doctors admitted my mom to the hospital and scheduled surgery for the following morning to place a drain tube into the mass to drain out any fluid or blood.

Tears began to slide down my face. Any hope for normalcy that weekend had been dashed by another emergency. Thinking back, I laugh at the selfish thoughts running through my head that day. Concern for my mother filled my mind, but so did the list of errands and cleaning I had planned for that weekend. The list on my phone to change air filters, replace burner trays, do laundry, and clean my neglected home now had no chance of getting accomplished.

Reluctantly, I entered the staff women's lunch determined to at least finish that part of my day before rushing home to pack a bag and meet my mom at the hospital for, presumably, a long weekend. During the time with my staff women, I vaguely mentioned that I had planned to clean that weekend after having been gone for most of the prior month caring for my mom.

There I was on Interstate 40 West again, the drive becoming so natural that I felt as if I could take my hands off of the steering wheel and my car would know exactly where to take me. Nancy passed the torch back to me. So I found myself back on the sixth floor enjoying unhurried time once again with my mom. Around 3:00 a.m., some blood test results showed my mom's blood count was super low, which was not surprising because of her recent chemotherapy. She needed a blood transfusion before surgery the next morning. Since this was her very first blood transfusion, nurses monitored her more closely. They checked her blood pressure every five minutes for the duration of the transfusion. With fluorescent lights glaring at us, I was resigned to another sleepless night.

Mesmerized by the process, I pondered the reality that someone had donated the blood being pumped into my mom's body, essentially saving her life. At the time, it may have seemed a small measure for that person to give blood, but tonight, I was acutely aware of the magnitude of the gift of that pint of blood that would allow my mom to have the surgery as scheduled in mere hours. As I watched the red blood flow from the bag, down through the tube, and into my mom's body, I was struck by the stark similarity of it to the blood that Jesus shed on the cross. He gave His blood as a gift so that I might have a chance at life. Again I was seeing God's goodness to us in the little things like a blood transfusion to sustain my mom's life that night and in the major things like Christ shedding His blood to provide a way for us to have true and abundant life in Him. "Oh, taste and see that the Lord is good!" (Ps. 34:8).

The next morning, my mom was ready for the surgery. The procedure to insert the drain went well, and as tests were sent off to pathology to determine the nature of the mass, the patient nurses began to teach me how to clean the drain and care for my mom.

Knowing that I had now been awake for over thirty-six hours, Bert arrived to take the night shift so that I could return to Raleigh to shower and sleep. I called Nicole on my drive home to explain in detail the happenings of the last few days. While still on the phone, I parked my car, gathered my things, and went up to my house. Exhaustion ran threw me and delirium took over because when I turned on the lights and entered my bedroom, I gasped and told Nicole that I thought someone may have broken into my house and changed my comforter to the reversible side that I don't typically use. She laughed and told me to open my eyes and look around. As I followed her command, I began to notice that these so-called burglars not only made my bed but also did my laundry and left it folded neatly on my bed. My bathroom was spotless, and beautiful flowers stood in a vase on my bedside table. Tears filled my eyes, and I whispered to Nicole, "Who did this for me?"

She told me that some of the staff women who loved me had come and cleaned my house while I was at the hospital. I took some steps back and opened my eyes even more. Not just my bedroom—my entire house was spotless. Somehow, without my ever sharing the list on my phone, these women had also managed to change the air filters and buy new burner trays for my stove (two very specific things from my to-do list). I showered and drifted off to sleep that night with a keen sense that God really does see even the tiniest, most mundane details of my life. He cares about the things that I care about and loves me more deeply than I can imagine. Jehovah-Jireh, the God who Provides, had through the women on my staff team, reminded me that I am not alone and I am not forgotten.

After a good night's sleep in my freshly cleaned home, I returned to Chapel Hill. Reports showed that the mass most likely was a hematoma that simply needed to be drained—the best news we could have received in this instance. Although we thought the drain was only temporary, it actually stayed with my mom for another eight weeks because my mom's body was unable to heal itself due to the chemo. True to form, my mom never complained, even though the drain was uncomfortable, inconvenient, and foul smelling. I knew that she didn't like it, and I knew she was disappointed every other week when we attended the appointment to remove it only to find out it had to stay, but through it all, she never complained.

By this point, I had learned to expect the unexpected twists and turns of this roller coaster ride, so I laughed one Tuesday when a weather report predicted eight inches of snow coming to Chapel Hill that Wednesday night. My mom and I had plans to drive to Chapel Hill on Thursday for another possible drain removal appointment and again on Friday for her fourth round of chemo. To many, this may seem like no big deal. Not to me. I don't do snow. I don't even like to walk outside in half an inch of snow, much less drive in eight inches of it with my very weak and sick mother. A sick feeling washed over me as I pictured my car stuck in the snow or off the road in a ditch with my mom in the passenger seat unable to walk with me for help. The planner in me kicked in, knowing that I would do whatever it took to get my mom to those appointments that week, and courage built up inside of me to face the snow. First, I called my mom and told her that she needed to prepare to leave on Wednesday and not return until Friday. I told her to pack up enough medical supplies and medicines for three days away from home. Next, I called hotels in Chapel Hill until I finally found a vacancy just five miles from UNC Hospitals. They even gave us a medical discount. Then, Wednesday morning, I left Raleigh and drove the hour to Goldsboro to get my frail mother, and together we drove the hour and a half back toward Chapel Hill. I was determined to make this work. As I got her into the hotel room, along with all our bags and medical supplies, I was amazed at the amount of supplies it took to care for her needs. I stocked the hotel room with food for the next few days.

Sleep did not come that night as I watched the simultaneously beautiful and dreadful snow falling steadily outside our hotel window. The next morning, as predicted, eight inches of snow had fallen. I bundled up and anxiously stomped my way out to my car hours before the drain appointment. I scraped the ice and brushed the snow off of my windshield. I prayed while I worked that God would somehow give me the courage and the ability to drive my car to the hospital, unsure if I could even get out of the parking lot, much less onto the main road. Carrying a light bag of supplies, I helped my mom from the hotel room, across the snow and into the car. Cautiously—more like scared to death—I pulled out from the hotel and inched the car and my precious passenger to the appointment. Finally, after what seemed like a lifetime of white-knuckled driving, we arrived safely to the hospital, only to find out that most of the nurses and doctors had spent the night there for fear of not being able to make it back that morning.

Although the doctors could not remove the drain tube that day as we had hoped, we did enjoy a warm meal in the hospital before hesitantly heading back to the hotel. My confidence grew as we repeated the process the next morning, returning to the hospital for chemo. The best thing happened that day: during chemo, Dr. Kim told us that, according to my mom's blood work, her tumor marker numbers had dropped significantly. Before her original surgery to remove the tumor, her numbers had been at 180. Now the test showed them at 3.6.

As we faced another few weeks of grueling recovery from the chemo, we could finally see a light at the end of the tunnel. We could feel it. "Oh, taste and see that the Lord is good!" (Ps. 34:8).

6

A LIGHT AT THE END OF THE TUNNEL

As EXPECTED, THE week following chemo proved hard for my mom. Frail and weak, she could barely get up to go to the bathroom during those recovery days without help. Even with help, she often had to stop in route to the bathroom to hang her head down on a chair back to catch her breath or steady herself before finishing the short steps left to get from the couch to the bathroom. Determined, she set the goal of attending my niece's birthday party on Saturday (just eight days after chemo). Friends prayed that she would be able to attend, and as the day arrived, mom felt well enough to make the hour-long trip to Greenville for the party. She sat on the couch at Bert's house, proud to be there and so proud of her sweet eight-year-old granddaughter!

A few weeks later, my mom went back to the hospital for another drain appointment, a CT scan of the drain site, and a measurement of the hematoma that had been draining. At long last, the doctors determined that it was time to remove the drain. Eight weeks of emptying and cleaning the drain and smelling its odor finally came to an end. Hope, celebration, and excitement spread across my mom's face.

With the drain removed, the tumor marker numbers in the normal range, and the sixth—and hopefully final—chemo treatment just weeks away, a newfound hope began to stir in my heart. I am generally a very cautious person when it comes to hope, so much so that my ability to hope or dream is often overshadowed by fear of disappointment. I figure it is better to have low expectations and to be surprised, than have high expectations and to be let down. But this season surfaced some of the deepest longing I had ever known and a desire to truly hope to see my mom cancer free: a cancer survivor and no longer a cancer patient. So I hoped like I had never hoped before. Simultaneously, I reminded myself that God is still good, no matter the outcome.

On April 1, 2015, I wrote in my journal:

Lord, you are *good*. Regardless of the outcome of the hopes and dreams for the "not yets" in our lives, you remain good. Even when the pains and hurts and brokenness of this world seem to consume us, *still* you are good! Lord Jesus, I come to you, hoping and pleading that you would allow this last chemo treatment for mom to remove any last microscopic bits of cancer in her. Lord, we pray boldly that her scans would be clear at the end of this month. And Lord, we will give you all the glory for it.

I continued to process this idea of hope, remembering the story of Shadrach, Meshach, and Abednego in the book of Daniel. Refusing to bow down to false gods and faced with the fiery furnace, they confidently placed their hope in God, declaring, "Our God whom we serve is able to deliver us from the burning fiery furnace, and He will deliver us out of your hand, O king" (Daniel 3:17). And with equal confidence, they state, "But if not, be it known to you, O king, that we will not serve your gods or worship the golden image that you have set up" (Daniel 3:18). I love their confidence and their unwavering trust in the holy God. "But if not..." But if not, our God is still worthy of our faithfulness to Him. But if not, our God is still King. But if not, our God is still good. God doesn't always answer our prayers in the way that we think He should. But if not, He is still God! And He sees the bigger picture and knows what is best for us, far better than what we could hope for ourselves.

So, I finished out my journal entry that first day in April:

Jesus, thank you that you see, you know, and you love me deeply. Thank you that you haven't wasted this season for our family; you have drawn us closer to each other and closer to you. Lord, thank you for the beauty in pain, and thank you for the countless people who have rallied around us through prayer and serving our family. Jesus, would you receive all the glory! Would you continue to restore and revive Hope in my life? Hope for the "not yets," a willingness to hope for your deliverance from the fiery trials of life, but a humbleness to say, "but if not...you are still good—still Lord, still King!"

On April 10th, my mom went to her sixth, and hopefully final, chemo treatment. After the day-long treatment, she was asked to come around the corner into a special part of the chemo infusion room. It was her time to ring the bell. At UNC, patients would ring the "I finished chemo" bell upon finishing their last treatment. A cousin took a picture, and my mom's face glowed, an exuberant smile stretched from ear to ear, and her bald head—a result of her battle—was worn proudly and confidently. She was a picture of relief, victory, and accomplishment. Hope abounded in what had been the hardest, most grueling, and taxing race of her life. She crossed the finish line! Although the final "cancer free" declaration wouldn't come for three weeks, all the signs pointed in that direction. Our hearts soared as she rang that bell!

We headed home from the hospital that spring day full of hope and anticipating that my mom might be well enough to attend the annual women's dinner held at her church a few weeks later. This year, I had been asked to be the main speaker. Several weeks after her last chemo treatment and still a week before the final CT scan that would give us the answers we had been waiting for, we decided that my mom was well enough to attend the dinner with me. It was her first major public outing since her initial diagnosis six months earlier. Though still weak from the chemo, she was radiant and excited to be around her church family.

That night, I shared with the women details of our family's story as we faced this terrible disease and the truth of God's goodness in the midst of the horror. I talked about the character of God that stood true through the test of trials, how He is trustworthy and constant. I expressed hope, hope that my mom would be declared cancer free, and I asked them to pray with us to that end. I also explained my desire to trust the goodness of Jesus no matter the outcome.

Not long after the church dinner, I headed out for my summer assignment with Cru in Clearwater Beach, Florida. Saying good-bye to my mom was difficult, and tears flowed. I caravanned from North Carolina to Florida with my good friends and coleaders, and we stopped at Chick-Fil-A for lunch upon arriving in Clearwater. After ordering, my phone rang, and it was my mom. There, sitting on a bench outside of Chick-Fil-A in the sweltering Florida heat, I heard the words I had longed to hear for six months.

"I'm cancer free!" my mom cried.

Tears flooded from my eyes: hope fulfilled, longing fulfilled. "So this is what it feels like," I thought. Being thirty-five and single, I had experienced lots of unfulfilled, deep longing to be married and have a family of my own. I was used to hearing "no" or "not yet" from the Lord—until now.

As I sat on that bench, a series of memories flashed through my mind: the initial diagnosis, the fearful tears we had shed, endless trips to the hospital and sleepless nights with my mom, long days in the chemo room, caring for her during the tiring weeks following chemo, cleaning up after her when she couldn't hold back the nausea or hold her bowels long enough to make it to the toilet, shaving her head bald—a constant reminder of the cancer in her body—catching her and nearly carrying her when she passed out or was too weak to stand, watching her slender body waste away. Suddenly, all of those things were worth it—simply horrific steps on a marathon of running toward better health—and my mom had just broken through the finish line. Cancer free. Cancer survivor.

Romans 12:15 says, "Rejoice with those who rejoice, weep with those who weep." For months, our friends had been weeping with us, and now it was time to rejoice. I sent an update to my email list thanking my dear friends and prayer warriors for standing with us and interceding on our behalf. Now it was time to rejoice!

After two full months, we celebrated in July at Topsail Beach with our extended family. It was the thirty-sixth year in a row that we had all joined for a week at the beach together. This one was special, knowing all that my mom had battled through that year. With three different houses and four generations of cousins, we had a blast enjoying time together and sharing memories of years passed. To top it off, it was my birthday week, and having my mom present was the best birthday gift I could have ever received.

As the summer months continued to pass, hope, celebration, and relief continued to reign in our family. However, during these months, I began to realize that although my mom was declared physically cancer free, we all continued to mentally fear its return. Every strange thing that my mom experienced with her body in those summer months sent an alarm pulsing through each of us. "Could it be cancer again?" I can't imagine anyone going through the hell that my mom went through without being haunted by the possibility of cancer's return. My mom had lots of scares that summer—more than I'm sure she even admitted to us—but again and again, doctors told us that it was just her body healing from all that it had been through, particularly the intense and invasive initial surgery she had endured.

So we continued to trust, and my mom continued to push through the hard and uncomfortable symptoms she was experiencing. As she gained strength, my mom went back to work and church and began to experience life as she remembered it before the horror of cancer.

7

HOPE IN THE DARKNESS

I WISH THAT I could say the story ended there. My mom's strange and unpleasant symptoms continued and actually worsened in the months following that summer of celebration. The threat and fear of cancer hung thick in the air around us, but doctor after doctor assured us that her body was just changing and healing from all it had been through. My mom was determined to live with the uncomfortable and unpleasant things she was experiencing.

In the midst of this, I assumed she was probably miserable because she was honest with me about what was happening in and to her body, but she never complained. Not once. By the early fall, we knew that something had to be done to fix the problems my mom was having. Her oncologist agreed, and after several more scans and tests, he determined that she had a fistula (a small tear) somewhere with fluid leaking from her insides, causing the unpleasantness. Though the surgery would be invasive and require another long recovery, he agreed that it was time to go back in and see what could be done to help.

On September 30th, my mom was back in surgery. My dad, Bert, and I prayed for her, kissed her good-bye, and took up our role of waiting in the surgical waiting area. Though we were entertained for the first few hours by watching all sorts of fascinating people that day, more hours than we expected passed. We knew the surgery was complex, but we didn't expect it to last longer than a few hours. Afraid to get too far from the waiting room, Bert and I walked back and forth down the hall as another hour passed. The waiting room began to empty out as late afternoon approached. Still no word for us. Fear and worry crept in. Soon, we were the only ones left in the waiting room. I began to change seats every twenty minutes or so, moving my way around the waiting room, willing the time to pass by more quickly. Even the hospital volunteer for the day shut everything down and left. My dad, Bert, and I began to stare at one another wondering what was going on in the operating room on the other side of the wall.

Finally, the waiting room phone rang. I answered it the same as I had multiple times earlier that day, when it was for other families. This time I knew it was for us. A kind voice asked to speak to someone in the Malpass family. I let them know that I was Lynda's daughter. She told me that our family could step around the corner into the family consultation room, where the doctor would meet us momentarily. I'm sure the color drained from my face as I explained this to my dad and Bert. We had watched many times as families went into the consultation room, often coming out ashen and grief stricken. My dad shook his head, holding back the tears. We silently walked around and entered this small room with several chairs. There on the small table sat a box of tissues. Weary from the day of waiting and anxious about the outcome of the surgery, we waited silently, unable to look one another in the eye.

Dr. Kim entered the room and, before even sitting down, told us that my mom was out of surgery and doing well. For the first time in hours, I truly exhaled. Moments later, Dr. Kim told us that the cancer was back. Tears slid down my face, and I was unable to speak. My jaw hung open in disbelief. Honestly, I don't think this scenario had crossed my mind. I had thought of many other horrible things that he could tell us that day, but since my mom had recently had a clear CT scan, the return of cancer was the furthest thing from my thoughts. I don't remember Dr. Kim's details that day—something about her losing a lot of blood, having multiple blood transfusions, and lots of adhesions that made the surgery much more difficult and lengthy than originally expected. He continued to talk while my dad, Bert, and I sat in shock. Then, almost as quickly as he entered the room, he left.

The tears came on strong. Many thoughts warred for attention in my mind: "how can this be happening," "I am too weary to go through this again," "where is God," and "life just seemed to get back to semi-normal for all of us." On and on and on. We were being thrown back onto the roller coaster, only this time I was not ready. I didn't think I could do this again. "Oh Lord, please help me."

Unsuccessfully, I tried to compose myself to walk back out to the surgical waiting room where we waited to see my mom. "Her cancer has returned." Those four words flipped my world upside down again. Dread, fear, and anger built up in my heart.

Another hour or so passed, and it was now dark outside. While we waited, we contacted a few friends and family with the shocking, sad news. A nurse came to get us and told us that we could see my mom in recovery. She did not yet know of the cancer's return, so we were supposed to somehow be upbeat and cheery and welcome her back from surgery. We prayed she wouldn't see the bloodshot fear in our eyes. My mom's intuition and perception, even while still drugged and coming out of the anesthesia, told her something wasn't quite right, and even though she asked, we deferred answering and told her we would talk later.

Late that night, before Bert and my dad left the hospital (it was my night to spend the night), we gathered around her bed back on the sixth floor and told her the cancer had returned. Defeat clouded my mom's eyes. I could tell that familiar war of thoughts was raging in her mind.

Neither of us slept much that night. Not only was cancer looming over us again, but my mom also faced a grueling recovery. The newly stitched incision, nearly a foot long, was a clear reminder of the day's surgery that left her scraped and sore, both inside and out.

Rain fell steadily most of the week following my mom's surgery—a constant, drenching rain flooding much of North Carolina. For days, I sat in the chair in my mom's hospital room watching the rain hit the window and then quickly slide down the glass, mirroring the tears that often slid down my cheeks that week. A suffocating grief over-whelmed me. At times, I felt that I could not catch my next breath. I never expected her cancer to return so suddenly. The rain continued. My tears continued. My heart slowly broke as I faced reality.

One afternoon, a knock on the door drew me from my grief. A florist delivery arrived with multiple flower arrangements for my mom. One in particular was stunning, by far the most beautiful flower arrange-ment I had ever seen. Artistic, curvy sticks framed bright coral roses, orange gerbera daisies, blue hydrangeas, yellow million stars, and crisp white lilies. I read the card, but the name wasn't familiar. So I read it aloud to my mom, and she was also unsure of the sender. We were both perplexed. Not until hours later did I finally realize that the sender was the lady who waxed my mom's eyebrows at the hair salon. Amazingly, someone who my mom saw for about five minutes every few months sent us the most exquisite flower arrangement I had ever seen. As I set the arrangement on the hospital room windowsill, as strange as it may sound, the Lord shifted my attitude and perspective. I posted a photo online and included this caption:

I have spent much of the last few days looking at the raindrops rolling down this window. They have been a perfect backdrop for how I am feeling these days—for those of you who don't know yet, my mom's cancer has returned. Then a friend sent these gorgeous flowers that I began to see as I watched the raindrops. They remind me that there is beauty in the sadness. Beauty in the grief. Beauty in the suffering. I'm trying to find gratitude and beauty in the little things. And mostly I am grateful for the Beautiful One who knows our situation and sees every raindrop and every tear and cares for our family deeply in our sadness.

I'm sure that our friend Chris, who waxes our eyebrows, could never have imagined the impact those flowers would have on us. Something about their beauty transformed my heart. Still today, the picture of those flowers (now the backdrop on my phone and the cover for this book) reminds me of beauty in suffering. However, even this renewed perspective couldn't fend off the anger and deep, deep sadness taking up residence in my heart.

My journal entry from October 13th captured some of my heart's cry:

I am so angry. So hurt. So sad. Four months cancer free, and it returns. The grief and sadness feels suffocating at times; I can't imagine life without my mom, and yet it feels like God is asking me to give her up. And I can't reconcile how a good God would ask that. I want to believe truth about God's promises, but it is hard to believe truth these days. Oh Jesus, help my unbelief. I am angry that the cancer has returned—angry at the situation, at the disease, at life, and at a God who would allow it to return. I am angry that my mom has to go through this fight again before she even had a chance to celebrate beating cancer the first time. I am angry that I will once again pull away from my team, my ministry, and my life in Raleigh to help care for her. I am angry because I feel like our family needs relief, yet our circumstances are unrelenting. Oh Jesus, would you relent? Would you heal her body? Would she defy all odds and be the one with ovarian carcinosarcoma who outlives five years cancer free? Oh Jesus, would you heal her? My heart is hurting—the pending loss seems unbearable. And as I look around me, everyone else's life looks perfect. I can't help but ask, why me, why us, why her, why this? Lord, I feel so alone. My mom is the main person I talk to on a day-to-day basis—if she is gone, who will care about my day to day? I feel more alone and single than I have in a while. I need someone to share this grief with—someone to help carry the burden. I suppose I need you, Christ, yet fear keeps me from wanting to truly enter in, because it is hard to trust you right now. Lord, give me a thankful heart, a servant's heart, a trusting heart. I need you, Jesus.

Throughout the fall, I read a book called *Respectable Sins* with some of the senior girls at NC State. In one chapter, the author wrote of moving from an attitude of victim to an attitude of stewardship. Something about this paradigm shift struck me. I realized that I had been looking at life through the lens of a victim—a victim of this vicious disease slowly sucking the life from the person to whom I felt closest. With a desire to point others to Christ, I began to pray that God would move my heart's attitude from one of victim to one of stewardship. He brought Lamentations 3:21–24 to my mind, and I copied it in my journal on October 19th:

But this I call to mind, and therefore I have hope; The steadfast love of the Lord never ceases, His mercies never come to an end; they are new every morning; great is your faithfulness. "The Lord is my portion," says my soul, "therefore I will hope in Him." (Lam 3:21-24)

In my journal, I wrote my own thoughts on the subject:

> Lord Jesus, I do want to grieve well this news about mom. But instead of wallowing in pity and feeling like our family continues to be the victims of bad and painful circumstances, Lord, I want to be a wise steward of every day you've given me on the earth—even the painful ones, even the ones where my mom has cancer, and even the ones where my fragility is overwhelming and from moment to moment I don't know if I will make it through the next sentence without choking up. I want to steward this life well; I want to be a light to those who don't know you. I want to be an encouragement to those who do. Jesus, would you give me the strength and the courage to shift from victim to steward? Would you reveal to me how you would have me steward my life in this season?

Trusting God continued to be a struggle as I prayed for the ability to move from victim to steward. I continued to pray, "I believe, help my unbelief" (Mark 9:24).

8

HOPE IN HEAVEN

IN OCTOBER 2015, exactly one year after my mom's initial "suspicious" CT scan, I found myself back at Cru's annual conference for campus leaders in our region. Feeling fragile and brokenhearted, I knew I needed to be surrounded by a great community of people who loved and cared for me.

One day during a break in our meetings, I found myself in what started out as a rather surface-level conversation with a long-time colleague. Hank Marshman is a well-known "hero of the faith," mentor, and father figure to many in our Cru family. Hank was aware I was transitioning out of a summer role I'd held for over a decade, so he acknowledged the sadness I must be experiencing with that transition. I gave a half-hearted laugh and said that while I was sad about that season in my life coming to a close, there was so much more going on and so much more to grieve. Hank pressed in and began to ask some more questions, and eventually I revealed that my mom's cancer had returned. I explained that even though I knew my mom was a follower of Jesus and that God was with us, I was struggling to believe that God was good. Tears flowed rather unexpectedly. While this was becoming normal behavior for me, to this acquaintance who knew nothing of my mom's cancer, I'm sure I seemed quite fragile. I'm sure Hank wasn't expecting our passing conversation to take this turn.

Instead of shrinking away from the awkwardness, like many might have chosen to do, Hank began speaking into the depths of my heart and soul in a way that can only be explained as the Lord speaking through him. In our conversation, he shared with me a story about a cruise that he and his wife had recently been given. He described the extravagant ship, the delicious food, and the joy of running into old friends on the ship, a chance encounter that allowed them to spend the day laughing, sharing stories, and playing volleyball together. He described the second night as better than the first! The food was even better than the previous night—something he could not have even imagined. He told me how the ship stopped each day at a new, beautiful island location—each day more exquisite and beautiful than the one before, which left him wondering if that location might be the most beautiful place on Earth. The story went on, and tears continued to stream down my face. Hank went on to make a beautiful comparison between his story and the reality of Heaven. He gently reminded me that God is indeed good, and because my mother knew Jesus, she would get to experience something so much greater than his description of the cruise. He reminded me that God is indeed good because cancer is the only hell that my mom would ever have to face.

"Oh, taste and see that the Lord is good!" (Ps. 34:8). Hank's reminder of God's goodness and gentle encouragement made a huge impact in this season of my life. It also prompted a conversation that I knew I needed to have with my mom.

For twelve months, my mom and I focused on two things: fighting cancer and staying strong. Determined to stay strong for one another, not once did we verbalize our fears or sadness. I kept my tears and "freak out weeping in the fetal position" moments private, which was painful because I always shared everything with her. In other "freak out weeping in the fetal position" moments in my life, she would have been my first call. Sadness crept in as I realized our relationship had changed in this season because we were working so hard to protect one another.

After my conversation with Hank, I knew I not only wanted to share the Heaven analogy with her, but I also wanted to share with her from the depths of my heart. I wanted her to know how great the loss would be in my life if something were to happen to her. One Friday afternoon, I drove to Goldsboro planning to arrive before my dad got home from work. Finally, after months of standing strong, we let our guard down and shared our deepest fears. We cried deep, agonizing tears and talked about the reality of what may be happening. My mom assured me that she was ready for Heaven if that is what the Lord wanted for her. We talked about fears: my fear of not having her in my life and her fear that her grandchildren might one day forget her. Our conversation led to a sweet and knowing peace. We made an agreement not to waste time protecting each other and agreed to share openly and honestly. We also decided to capture these fleeting moments with a family photoshoot before her chemo treatments started back.

The next day, my mom begged me to take her shopping. I feared her body wouldn't be able to hold up, especially because she was still recovering from a major surgery, and yet I realized that she might not have many more opportunities to shop. Nothing compared to the joy she got from buying things for other people, especially her grandchildren. Since Christmas was just around the corner, I knew she wanted nothing more than to go Christmas shopping. So I agreed and told my dad I was taking her out. Although his eyes told me he disapproved, I promised him we would stay in Target for only one hour and then I would bring her home to rest.

Shopping with my mom that day was something I will never forget. Like a woman on a mission, my mom grabbed stuff left and right, throwing it in the cart. Weak but smiling widely as her cart rapidly grew, she at times didn't know what or for whom the items may be. In just under an hour, our cart bursting at the seams, we checked out, and I drove her home. I got her settled on the couch and then unloaded the countless bags. My dad's eyes grew wider and wider as my mom's smile grew. She couldn't wait to show him all that she had found. Later, my dad confessed that taking her shopping and seeing her smile like that again was the right decision after all.

Recovery from surgery continued, and we began to gear up for another six rounds of chemo. This time around, the doctors tried a new mix of drugs recommended for cancer recurrence. The first day of the next round neared, and fears mixed with memories of the horror of the last round. Were we really ready to do this again?

Just before chemo began again, our family enjoyed a wonderful afternoon in a park in Raleigh with a photographer. Some friends helped us schedule the time and, as a gift to our family, even covered the cost. The talented photographer captured sweet and priceless memories for us with pictures of our entire family and individual pictures of each of us with my mom. Every single photograph captured a cherished memory for our family. Afterward, even though mom was quite weak, she joined the family at Noodles and Co. for an early dinner before returning to Goldsboro. The afternoon was filled with laughter and smiles, an outing that encouraged my mom in the face of the next grueling round of chemo.

I copied several verses in my journal during these days leading up to restarting chemo:

The Lord is the strength of His people; He is the saving refuge of His anointed. (Ps. 28:8)

I lift my eyes up to the hills. From where does my help come? My help comes from the Lord, who made heaven and earth.

He will not let your foot be moved; He who keeps you will not slumber. Behold, He who keeps Israel will neither slumber nor sleep. The Lord is your keeper; the Lord is your shade on your right hand. The sun shall not strike you by day, nor the moon by night. The Lord will keep you from all evil; He will keep your life. The Lord will keep your going out and your coming in from this time forth and forevermore. (Ps. 121)

More than that, we rejoice in our sufferings, knowing that suffering produces endurance, and endurance produces character, and character produces hope, and hope does not put us to shame, because God's love has been poured into our hearts through the Holy Spirit who has been given to us. (Rom. 5:3–5)

For I consider that the sufferings of this present time are not worth comparing with the glory that is to be revealed to us. (Rom. 8:18)

No, in all these things we are more than conquerors through Him who loved us. For I am sure that neither death nor life, nor angels nor rulers, nor things present nor things to come, nor powers, nor height nor depth, nor anything else in all creation, will be able to separate us from the love of God in Christ Jesus our Lord. (Rom. 8:37–39)

We have this as a sure and steadfast anchor of the soul, a hope that enters into the inner place behind the curtain, where Jesus has gone as a forerunner on our behalf. (Heb. 6:19–20)

Rejoice always, pray without ceasing, give thanks in all circumstances; for this is the will of God in Christ Jesus for you. (1 Thess. 5:16–18)

As November 20th arrived, we were ready. I drove my mom back to Chapel Hill for another day in the gynecological oncology infusion room. Compared to the all-day affair of her last chemo treatments, this new round would take only a few hours each time. The new drug, Doxil, was known for sometimes causing a harsh reaction upon first interacting with the body. We were warned, signed some papers, and didn't think much of it.

As the drug took its first few drips into my mom's bloodstream that day, alarm paralyzed me as I watched my mom turn beet red, struggle to breathe, and almost pass out. Within seconds, there were more nurses and doctors standing over us than I had ever seen in the infusion room. Stuck in a corner chair beside my mom's chemo chair with no room to move out of the way, I stared at the chaos swirling around me. Quickly and calmly, a nurse took my mom's lunch from her lap and set it on top of my lunch, which was already sitting in my lap. They laid my mom back, got the equipment in place, and began to take her vitals while shooting different medicines into her system. Still stunned, I sat frozen as doctors and nurses leaned over me to work on my mom. Within ten to fifteen minutes, her color returned, her breathing steadied, and her vitals began returning to normal. What was supposed to be a quick and easy trip turned into a six-hour, scary ordeal. After a few hours of waiting for my mom's body to recover, the doctors slowly began the drip again. This time, my mom's body tolerated the drug much better.

Over the course of the next several days, we watched the chemo take a terrible toll on my mom's body. She was weak, weary, and once again needed help with most basic tasks. Embracing the journey ahead, I created a new color-coded calendar to keep track of this next season of treatments, and together we were determined to take up the fight once again.

9

A NEW PATH

A FEW WEEKS AFTER that chemo treatment, with one of my mom's sister-cousins in place to care for her, I was back in Raleigh with my staff team in one of our long and busy end-of-the-semester planning weeks. This week included extra meetings to plan for the next semester coupled with countless extra final activities to say good-bye to graduating seniors. Late one Monday night, as I prepared my house to host the staff meeting the next morning, my mom called and told me that something was wrong. She had not felt well for several days, which I knew, but earlier that day, she began to experience similar symptoms to those she had before her surgery in September. This time, they were worse. This time, instead of experiencing leaking from her insides where the fistula had been, the leaking was coming directly from her bowel, and every time she sat down or stood up, gravity did its work and made the leaking even worse, causing a mess to clean up. She sounded miserable and was in a lot of pain. She felt unable to get in the car to get to the hospital in Chapel Hill. That night, Bert and I insisted we call an ambulance to transport her to Chapel Hill. For some reason, she was adamant that she wait until the morning and call her doctor to see what she should do. When morning came, her doctor told her to come to the hospital immediately.

Tuesday morning came, and before my coworkers arrived at my house, I packed my stuff for what I knew would probably be another long stay at the hospital. I decided to leave in the middle of the staff meeting to get to the hospital just before my parents. Deep in my heart, I knew that something was very wrong and that the news was not good. I arrived at the hospital about ten minutes before my parents, in time to find a wheelchair for my mom. As I met my parents under the canopy at the entrance to the women's hospital, my breath caught in my throat. My mom looked sicker than I had ever seen her. She could barely stand up, her face was gray and ashen, and her typically vibrant smile was absent. My dad gave me a knowing look. He too thought she looked sicker than ever before. I rolled my mom's wheelchair up to the second floor gyneco-logical oncology offices, as my dad quickly parked the car. I checked my mom in, and we waited. We knew that we wouldn't be able to see Dr. Kim, my mom's head oncologist, because he was usually in surgery on Tuesdays. Gratitude and relief washed over us when we saw one of our favorite other doctors on her oncology team, Dr. Sullivan, walk into the examination room. She had been present at all of my mom's surgeries and a face of sweet encouragement in all of our hospital stays.

Kind and gentle, seeming to empathize with the hell my mom was experiencing, Dr. Sullivan examined her and let us know that there did seem to be a tear in my mom's bowel. She said that they would need to admit her immediately and would most likely need to perform sur-gery again. She talked to us briefly about the remedy that would most likely include an ostomy, resulting in a small bag that would attach to my mom's intestines and then hang on the outside of her body to catch waste that would come from her body. At this point, an ostomy bag sounded wonderful compared to the symptoms my mom was experiencing, so we were anxious to move forward with the surgery.

Late into the night, a transport employee came to take my mom for a CT scan. The scan would show the doctors the exact location of the tear in her bowel. Early the next morning, Dr. Kim came in to see us and discuss next steps. Groggy from an uncomfortable night on the vinyl pullout chair, I struggled to think clearly and hear what he was saying. Slowly, I began to hear his words and notice the grim look on his face. I quickly reached for my phone and began recording his words for my dad and Bert. I am so grateful that I recorded that conversation—a conversation that changed everything.

Dr. Kim told us that after reading the CT scan from the night before, he could see that the cancer was growing and spreading fast. It appeared that the chemo from several weeks earlier had not helped at all. He told us that we had a choice to make. Option one: we could continue chemo with hopes that something would change (though that didn't seem likely). This option meant that my mom would have to put up with the horrific symptoms she was experiencing from the leaking bowel. Option two: we could stop the chemo treatments, have the surgery to get the ostomy bag and stop the current symptoms, and then seek hospice care for quality of life in my mom's final days. It would not be possible to continue chemo and to perform the surgery. It was one or the other.

There are moments in life when it seems that you are looking in from some far off place. Sounds seem muffled, and everything seems to be happening in slow motion. This was one of those moments. I couldn't believe what I was hearing. Every hope I had for my mom to beat the cancer was being stripped away. My mind was reeling. My mom was silent. Tears streamed down both of our faces. As Dr. Kim was still talking, I remember thinking that I should come up with questions to ask him. But I couldn't think of any. I wracked my brain for what I thought

Bert or my dad might ask if they were in the room, but all I could think about was that my mom was dying. "Think, Cam, think," I told myself.

Finally, I came up with some questions to ask about our options, the ostomy surgery and recovery, what he would do if his mom or wife were in the same situation. To make sure I was hearing correctly, I asked him to confirm that there was nothing more they could do, that the cancer was terminal, and that she only had a few months to live.

As Dr. Kim shut the large, heavy hospital room door behind him, my mom and I wept. We wept for the words we had just heard, for the deep sadness in both of our hearts, for the impending loss, and for the short time left ahead together. My mom asked me to pray, so with sobs catching my breath every few words, I prayed. First, I thanked God, because that is what His Word tells us to do; then, I thanked Him for my mom's life. I thanked Him for the hope of eternity. I thanked Him for the reunion that my mom would one day soon have with Him and with other loved ones who had gone before. I prayed for wisdom as we moved forward with decisions and, finally, for the courage to call my dad and Bert.

Then came the phone calls. I asked a nurse if I could use a private conference room on the sixth floor to make some phone calls. She led me there and put a note on the door so that I would have privacy. I first called Bert because I had no idea how to tell my dad any of what Dr. Kim had just said. I asked Bert through tears to find a place at work he could talk. Then, slowly between sobs, I tried to explain to him what Dr. Kim had said. Bert and I cried together and talked about how to move forward when it seemed that all hope for healing was gone. We had to decide how to tell my dad. We didn't want him to drive from Goldsboro knowing the truth. So we decided just to ask him to meet us at the hospital but not really tell him why. Bert left work and headed to Chapel Hill. I called my dad and told him that Dr. Kim had come in and given us lots of options about next steps and that I needed him to come join Bert and me so that we could make some decisions as a family. Somehow, I didn't cry during that conversation with my dad.

It was still fairly early in the morning when Bert arrived. My dad arrived an hour or so later. The nurses gave us space that day, and we sat as a family for hours in that hospital room, tears and deep sadness joining us as we faced reality. We talked about the options, but from the start, it was clear which choice we needed to make. My mom would have no quality of life without the ostomy. She couldn't sit or stand without her bowels literally gushing out from her. If the chemo was not working, we didn't want her final days to be marked by treatments and their side effects.

A fighter, my mom's greatest internal wrestle that day was to choose to stop the chemo. Our family agreed that we weren't giving up. We were just switching to a new path; choosing to stop chemo didn't signify failure but instead meant that we were changing gears. We had a new focus now: quality of life.

I remember that day—the day the doctor told me that my mom was dying in the next few months—being the saddest day of my life up to that point. We went through many tissues that day as we made countless phone calls to deliver the horrible news. But I also remember that day being a day filled with hope. As we camped out in that hospital room, we talked about truth and spoke hope into one another's souls. We reminded one another that our time here on Earth isn't the end; for the believer in Christ, a better day awaits. We grieved that day—oh, how we grieved! But we did not grieve like those with no hope.

In the days that followed, the Lord brought sweet Scripture to my mind to help me cope and to remind me of truth:

If we live, we live to the Lord, and if we die, we die to the Lord. So then, whether we live or whether we die, we are the Lord's. (Rom. 14:8)

So we do not lose heart. Though our outer nature is wasting away, our inner nature is being renewed day by day. For this slight momentary affliction is preparing us for an eternal weight of glory beyond all comparison, as we look not to the things that are seen but to the things that are unseen. For the things that are seen are transient, but the things that are unseen are eternal. (2 Cor. 4:16–18)

For in this tent we groan, longing to put on our heavenly dwelling, if indeed by putting it on we may not be found naked. For while we are still in this tent, we groan, being burdened—not that we would be unclothed, but that we would be further clothed, so that what is mortal may be swallowed up by life. He who has prepared us for this very thing is God, who has given us the Spirit as a guarantee. So we are always of good courage. We know that while we are at home in the body we are away from the Lord, for we walk by faith, not by sight. Yes, we are of good courage, and we would rather be away from the body and at home with the Lord. So whether we are at home or away, we make it our aim to please Him. (2 Cor. 5:2–9)

But we see Him who for a little while was made lower than the angels, namely Jesus, crowned with glory and honor because of the suffering of death, so that by the grace of God He might taste death for everyone. (Heb. 2:9)

10

THE BEGINNING OF THE END

WE WERE SENT home from the hospital for about a week before the ostomy could be scheduled. One day during that week, I received a text message from my mom's best friend, Marsha, a teacher at the school where my mom worked. Marsha asked me what I would think about some of the teachers coming by and Christmas caroling one night that week. At first, I thought it wouldn't work. My mom couldn't come to the door, and she still couldn't stand up without an incredible mess. I shared my concerns with Marsha, and she suggested that maybe they could come to the back porch, where my mom could remain lying on the couch but could still see out the glass doors and windows that stretched the length of the back of our house. I agreed, and we set the date. I wanted to surprise my mom, so I didn't mention it to her, but I did mention it to my dad. In my head, I pictured maybe fifteen to twenty teachers stopping by.

The night arrived, and my dad and I kept grinning at one another, knowing that my mom would be touched by the gesture. I began to see car lights in front of our house. It was time! Only the cars continued to gather. Then the WCDS bus pulled up, and people piled out. I stared in disbelief out the front room window as not just teachers but also students, families, and alumni gathered in front of our house. My dad and I began to cry as we saw hundreds of people who loved my mom gathering to show her they cared and to sing Christmas carols to her, but also to say farewell. As the group began to make its way to the back of our house, I went and whispered to my mom to look outside. My dad opened the French doors wide at the back of the house and turned on all of the floodlights. My mom asked me what was happening and I told her that some people wanted to sing carols to her. She asked me if it was our church friends. I said, "No, mom, it's the school."

Immediately, her tears flowed. As our backyard filled with countless people whom she had loved and served well through the years, they gave back. That night my mom was perhaps as honored and touched as she had ever been. She wept as they sang. At the end of the last song, they all yelled that they loved her. It was a precious moment that my mom carried with her for her remaining days. People don't often get to see this kind of outpouring of love, since it usually happens after their death, but that night my mom witnessed a fitting, touching, and well-deserved tribute. She had willingly given her all for years to this school and its families. And that night, they gave back to her. "Oh, taste and see that the Lord is good!" (Ps. 34:8).

Two days later, we left for Chapel Hill for the ostomy surgery with hopes to be home by Christmas. We also knew that, according to what the doctors predicted for a recovery time, we might be spending Christmas at UNC Hospitals. My dad, brother, sister-in-law, and I sat around my mom's hospital room all day. Friends visited on and off throughout the day to break up the waiting. I was glad that we decided not to wait in the uncomfortable surgical waiting room this time.

The surgery went well, and in the days that followed, our family sat through training times to learn how to care for, empty, and change my mom's ostomy bag. We learned about which food was okay for my mom to eat and how to determine proper portion sizes. Living with an ostomy bag is a change in lifestyle. Although we knew it would be short, we wanted my mom's quality of life for the time left to be the best possible.

We were thrilled to leave the hospital before Christmas and celebrate Christmas together home in Goldsboro. My mom's final Christmas. It was sweet and simple, full of love, moments of tears, and moments of laughter. We did our best to make this Christmas, though final, as normal as possible. My mom soaked it in. I could read in her eyes that she was cherishing each moment.

Around Christmas, we also began hospice. Our hospice nurse, Sheree, became a dear friend and confidant for my mom. My mom trusted her, as did our family. I was surprised at how amazing she was; she put us at ease when our family was facing the scariest, most unknown time of our lives. We looked forward to the days when Sheree would come. She cared deeply for my mom and was always a calming and reassuring presence in our house.

December 30th brought a sadness in our house. It was the anniversary of my grandfather's death. As I reflected on his life and the year following his death, I couldn't help but think about my mom's coming reality. She would soon join my grandfather in the arms of Jesus. Hope filled my heart. John 14:1–3 says, "Do not let your hearts be troubled. You believe in God; believe also in me. My Father's house has many rooms; if that were not so, would I have told you that I am going there to prepare a place for you? And if I go and prepare a place for you, I will come back and take you to be with me that you also may be where I am." Gratitude for this truth filled my soul. Because my mom had a relationship with Jesus, she would soon go to the very place that He had prepared for her.

Fatigue and exhaustion began to build in me during those days. The amount of care my mom needed grew daily as her body was declining. I was literally watching my mom whither away, as pound after pound fell from her body and as her strength quickly dissipated. She experienced additional pain and nausea as she recovered from the ostomy surgery. Perhaps the cancer was spreading and causing these symptoms. Our greatest prayer became for her to not suffer, and countless friends joined us in this.

The nonstop, day-and-night care for my mom was wearying. Thankfully, my mom's sister-cousins wanted time with her and scheduled to come. This gave me a few days back in Raleigh each week. I made Sheree promise to tell me when the time was drawing near and I should stay in Goldsboro permanently.

On January 15th, my mom had her final appointment in Chapel Hill with Dr.Kim. It was a follow-up appointment from the ostomy surgery. Earlier that day, I had lunch in Raleigh with my good friend Kalynn. I set an alarm on my phone, and when it went off, I told Kalynn that I had to leave so that I could beat my parents to the hospital and get a wheelchair ready for my mom. Kalynn asked me briefly about the wheelchair, letting me know that she didn't realize my mom needed a wheelchair now. I flippantly remarked that she couldn't do all of the walking in the hospital and that although we didn't yet need a wheelchair at home, we would soon have to look into it. I went on my way and met my parents at the hospital.

Our appointment with Dr. Kim was quick. Finality and sadness hung heavy in the examination room. Everything related to my mom's ostomy seemed to be going well. He suspected that her pain and nausea would subside as her body continued to adjust from the surgery. He encouraged us to continue doing what hospice was telling us to do. And then he said good-bye and left the room. We all cried as he closed the door. I remember stepping out of the examination room briefly and seeing Barbara, one of the nurses we had gotten to know. She hugged me and said that she thought we were doing the right thing. She said she watched countless women go through chemo with trips back and forth to UNC in their final days. She thought spending our final days at home with hospice was the best for my mom. I cried on her shoulder knowing I would most likely not see her—or the halls of that clinic, or the chemo nurses to whom we had grown so close—again.

We walked out of the hospital that day, and I looked back at the large rotating circular front door. I had walked in and out of that door hundreds of times in the last year. UNC Hospitals had, in many ways, become a place of familiarity, comfort, and relief to our family. But that day, I knew I was walking out of those doors for the last time with my mom. It was sad and seemed so final. As I drove away with tears flooding down my face, I felt an overwhelming sense of gratitude. Gratitude for UNC Health Care. Gratitude for Dr. Kim, who I believe God used to give us another year with my mom. Gratitude for the amazing gynecological oncology team and chemo nurses. Gratitude for the sixth floor women's team, who made our stays there as painless as possible. Gratitude for all of the staff at UNC who walked with us on this journey. I left that day sad but forever grateful.

The following day in Goldsboro, my mom's legs began cramping, leaving her in excruciating pain. My dad had gone to the grocery store, and I was alone with my mom. She needed to go to the bathroom, but when I went to help her stand, she couldn't bear any weight on her legs. We didn't have a wheelchair at home, so I sat her back down on the couch. I knew that my dad should be home any minute. I told my mom she would have to wait because I wasn't strong enough to carry her on my own. My dad arrived and helped me carry her to the bathroom. Our changing reality dawned on us, and my dad and I shared a look—one of us needed to go out that day to buy a wheelchair. We got my mom back to the couch, and before we could make plans for where to purchase a wheelchair, the doorbell rang.

I opened the front door, and there stood my friend Kalynn. In front of her was a wheelchair filled with supplies we might need: Clorox wipes, toilet paper, Kleenex, paper towels, etc. I stood dumbfounded and whispered, "How did you know we needed a wheelchair today?"

Perplexed by my question, she said that after I left lunch with her the day before, she had called around to several different thrift stores and found this one for thirty dollars. She knew we would need it someday and just decided to bring it to us. She rolled it into the living room where my parents were, and my dad teared up. God had provided a wheelchair in the exact moment we needed one. "Oh, taste and see that the Lord is good!" (Ps. 34:8).

Later that day, my mom kept telling me that she wanted some flavored ice. It was January, and my mom was asking me for Hawaiian shaved ice. I would have given anything to meet all her requests those days, but I kept telling her that the Hawaiian shaved ice places were not open in the winter months. She told me for the next hour how she was just craving flavored ice. Again, the doorbell rang.

I went to the door and stood dumbfounded for the second time that day. Jamsie, one of my dad's best friends, was standing on our front porch with a box of Italian Ice. Again I uttered, "How did you know?"

Perplexed he said, "Well, I was just in the grocery store, saw this, and thought it might be refreshing for your mom, so I picked it up and brought it over."

We laughed, and I told my parents that whatever else we may need we better say it out loud that day, because at this rate who knows what God might want to provide for us!

My mom's leg cramps continued to worsen and we prayed that we would figure out how to remedy it. We tried giving her more potassium. We tried hot bath cloths and bottles filled with hot water pressed up against her legs. That evening, her best friend Marsha told us that her father-in-law, a doctor, used to give people Tums for cramps. We grabbed a bottle of Tums, and my mom began taking those frequently.

By that night, the cramps had subsided. "Oh, taste and see that the Lord is good!" (Ps. 34:8).

The rest of January and February were sweet times. My mom continued to decline, and so we cherished the moments left with her more and more. There were unusually warm days where I would wrap my mother in a blanket and push her down the street and around the neighborhood in her wheelchair. We had sweet conversations about the past, but also about her future and what awaited her in Heaven. She needed my help now to get into the wheelchair, so I would bend down with my knees to pick her up, and she would wrap her arms around me, hugging me tightly, until I swung her around to her wheelchair. I found myself trying to memorize everything about my mom. When I bathed her, I tried to memorize the freckles on her back. When we talked, I did my best to take mental pictures of her smile and her piercing blue eyes. I begged the Lord not to let me forget a thing about her. It was during these days that I also memorized the picture that my dad was painting for me, a lived-out faithfulness and devotion to my mom. The phrase "in sickness and in health, till death do us part" took on a whole new meaning for me as I watched my dad care for my mom through the worst of times. He never wavered in his devotion to her.

In mid-February, my mom's oxygen levels got super low, so she began using an oxygen machine. I spent many days watching my mom sleep, with the rhythmic hissing hums of the machine mixed with her soft snores. While she slept, I remember often looking out the back windows of my parents' house thinking, "The world will never be the same again." Everything I had ever known was crumbling down in front of me and all I could do was sit by and watch, trying to memorize every moment.

My mom began to have more pain in February and switched to morphine as her primary pain medicine. The morphine helped with the pain but also made the caregiving job even more involved. At times, my mom was so drugged that she was unable to do basic things for herself. My dad and I began to have to help her with emptying her ostomy bag, and at times, she needed help eating, drinking, and taking her pills.

In March, I began to carry my mom outside to sit in the sun. I'd lay her down in a zero-gravity outdoor lounge chair and line it with pillows. It was unseasonably warm, and she would sleep for hours out on the back patio in the sun. Every afternoon, friends would join us and memorize their own last moments with my mom. Though my mom's strength was fading quickly, her appetite remained and gave hope for more days to sit with her, more days to share time with her, and more times to feel her arms wrapped around me in a tight hug as I would transfer her to and from her wheelchair.

Though grateful for the time, I was also losing strength and energy fast, weary from the caregiving and wondering, with tinges of guilt, how much longer could I keep this up. Part of me wanted to keep caring for my failing mom forever, and part of me longed for a break for me, for my dad, and for her body. The battle of guilt and confusion in my heart was strong in those days. It's hard to explain—the very thing I dreaded most and couldn't imagine happening was the very thing that would bring relief to a seemingly unending situation.

11

THE HOMEGOING

O<small>N</small> W<small>EDNESDAY</small>, M<small>ARCH</small> 16th, I was in Raleigh meeting with two students at the Brueggers Bagel shop near campus. We ended our time, and I headed to my car, glancing at my phone to see if I had missed any calls or texts. There was a text from Sheree, the hospice nurse, asking me to call her when I was free. I hopped in my car and immediately dialed her number. Sheree had shared something personal with me the week before, and I just assumed she was calling to share more details about that. I didn't think it was anything serious. Instead, through tears, Sheree told me that my mom was entering "the transition" period and that she thought I should plan to come to Goldsboro for my mom's final days. I was shocked. One of the major signs of a patient entering that stage is that they stop eating, and my mom was still eating a lot. Sheree explained to me that every patient is different, so maybe my mom would keep her appetite until the end. Sheree said she expected my mom had maybe two weeks left to live.

I texted a couple of close friends and headed to my house in Raleigh. When I got home, I called my dad and Bert and told them through tears what Sheree had said. I needed to pack but also had a million things to do running through my head. I felt paralyzed, unsure what to do next. My best friend Nicole did what I would highly recommend for anyone with a close friend facing this kind of heartache: she showed up. Nicole and her four kids parked at my house, and her husband met her there and took all of the kids. She helped me think, made lists, and ran errands with me that I needed to do before I went home for the weeks that followed. She was there. It wasn't what Nicole said that day; in fact aside from crying with me I can't tell you what she said that day. She showed up, something she would do many more times in the days that followed.

For thirty-six years, my mom taught me how to live, and in those final weeks of her life, my mom taught me how to die. She was at peace and ready to go whenever the Lord called her Home. My pride for my mom swelled in those days. She showed us how to die with beauty and grace and without fear. Her smile was genuine in those final weeks. Though her body was wasting away, she had an indescribable joy and unrivaled confidence. I always pictured the dying as fearful and full of uncertainty. But my mom changed that for me. There was no uncertainty for her, because she was sure of her relationship with Jesus and her future reality as she passed from this life to the next.

For months, our church family and other friends in the community had been bringing us meals each night. The thing I heard from them over and over was that they were so blessed and encouraged to be around my mom—it wasn't sad for them either. And even in her last few weeks, this trend continued. She continued to be a blessing to the many friends and family who came in and out of our house.

Palm Sunday was four days after Sheree had made that phone call to me. We could tell my mom was declining quickly. So, not sure what Easter Sunday would bring, we decided to celebrate Easter as a family early. We planned a big meal and invited family to join us. We held an Easter egg hunt inside so that my mom could see and hear the joys of her grandchildren hunting and squealing over finding eggs and their hidden contents. The Easter season brought with it great hope. In the midst of tremendous grief, we were extremely expectant and excited for my mom. With Easter near, there was a very tangible reminder that Christ has defeated the grave and that, for those who believe in Him, death is not the end. The tomb is empty. He is risen indeed. "Oh, taste and see that the Lord is good!" (Ps. 34:8). He is so, so good.

One day during the next week, I got a text saying that there was something from Wayne Country Day School left for my mom on our front porch. I went outside and found a beautiful orchid and a note. I brought the note to my mom. As she read it, her eyes filled with tears, and her shoulders began to shake as she cried. It was a letter from the senior class at the school letting her know that for their class gift, they were giving money to have a plaque placed in the hallway honoring my mom's thirty-five years of service to the school. The letter read as follows:

Dear Mrs. Malpass,

It is my honor and pleasure to inform you that we, the Class of 2016, as our senior gift, have decided to affix a plaque in the new high school concourse in honor of your 35 years of service to Wayne Country Day School.

Your example of love, devotion, and service to our school is simply exemplary. We seniors want to commemorate you so that everyone who comes to our school can see that you are most treasured and appreciated. With gratitude and great affection, The Senior Class of 2016

Again, my mom was given the gift of experiencing a taste of the tributes and honors she would receive after her death.

On Easter Sunday, we knew that the end was drawing near. Transferring my mom to and from the wheelchair became like lifting dead weight. She no longer had the strength to help at all. In addition, she struggled to even hold her body up in a sitting position, so taking her to the bathroom was becoming a struggle. Lastly, she really began to struggle to swallow. She had the desire to eat, but getting the food from the plate into her mouth required assistance, and her ability to remember to swallow was fading. It was all part of the process. By this point, we had stopped all of her medicines except for the liquid morphine, because swallowing pills was too difficult.

The Monday morning after Easter, my dad and I met Sheree at the front door and told her that we were really struggling to care for my mom. We wanted to keep her at home, but transferring her was becoming impossible, and we were afraid of hurting her or ourselves in the process. We decided to get a hospital bed placed in her room and to have Sheree insert a catheter so that my mom wouldn't have to get out of the bed. She ordered the bed, and it arrived within the hour. We set it up near the windows in my parents' bedroom so that she could look outside and see the flowers that my dad had planted for her on the patio. We moved some of the chairs from our living room into the bedroom so that friends and family could sit with her.

By this time, my mom's cousins began to arrive. Some of them stayed with us around the clock; Janie and Judy took care of every need we could possibly have. They kept us fed, monitored visitors coming in and out of our house, and did more laundry than was necessary. Some days, I think they rewashed my towels before I even had a chance to use them after the previous wash!

On Tuesday afternoon, my mom grabbed my hands and began to cry. Through tears, she said good-bye to my dad, Bert, and me. She had instructions for each of us. She told us to take care of each other. And she told us that she loved us. She looked me straight in the eyes and told me, "Write that book."

This book you are reading is largely being written because it was one of my mother's last requests of me. I mentioned the idea of writing it months earlier, and she remembered that and challenged me in some of her final words to me to follow through on that dream. Her breathing was slowing, and we thought that was the end. Her spirit was ready, but her body was still hanging on. I prayed through sobs that Jesus would take her to be with Him, that He would end her suffering. We watched attentively for her breathing to stop, but it continued, labored and heavy.

The afternoon turned into night; we stayed close by her bed and watched her breathe. Around 11:00 p.m. Tuesday, Bert looked at me and asked me if I was going to go to sleep that night. I was torn. For the last few months, I had pictured my mom's final days, final moments, and final breath in my mind. Every time, I had pictured all of us surrounding her. I didn't want to miss it. But I also knew that if Bert and I stayed there, my dad would not go to sleep. So Bert and I decided that we would camp out in the room with my mom and dad but that we would plan to sleep, turn off the lights, and take turns keeping an eye on my mom's breathing. My dad agreed and fell asleep.

The next morning, as my mom went in and out of consciousness, she had one lucid moment when she looked at us. I asked her how she liked our family campout in her room last night. She responded with great effort and slurred words, "You didn't leave me." Then she smiled. I knew from that moment on that we would all stay in that room by her side. My sister-in-law joined us on Wednesday and got some sweet, lucid moments with my mom. My mom's brother was there. Countless cousins, friends, and neighbors were filling our house. My mom was surrounded by so much love.

Her repeated words to all of us and to all who came in to see her in those final days was "I love you." It was as if she was leaving us with many "I love you" deposits to hold us over in her absence for the time that would span between her Homegoing and our one day meeting the Lord and being reunited with her ourselves. I can still hear and feel her whispered "I love yous" from those weary days.

Wednesday evening we camped out again. Sometime Wednesday or Thursday, my mom's pain increased. The sounds of her crying out and moaning in pain were horrific. We increased her morphine to every hour; Bert diligently kept watch, and used his phone alarm to be sure not a minute too long passed between her timed doses.

When I served with Cru overseas, often my team sang the hymn "My Jesus I Love Thee." I still think about my time in Asia when I hear that song. The lyrics are as follows:

> My Jesus, I love Thee, I know Thou art mine;
> For Thee all the follies of sin I resign;
> My gracious Redeemer, my Savior art Thou;
> If ever I loved Thee, my Jesus, 'tis now.
>
> I love Thee because Thou hast first loved me,
> And purchased my pardon on Calvary's tree;
> I love Thee for wearing the thorns on Thy brow;
> If ever I loved Thee, my Jesus, 'tis now.
>
> I'll love Thee in life, I will love Thee in death,
> And praise Thee as long as Thou lendest me breath;
> And say when the death dew lies cold on my brow,
> If ever I loved Thee, my Jesus, 'tis now.
>
> In mansions of glory and endless delight,
> I'll ever adore Thee in heaven so bright;
> I'll sing with the glittering crown on my brow,
> If ever I loved Thee, my Jesus, 'tis now.

As I sat beside my mom in those final days, I remembered the lyrics, "And say when the death dew lies cold on my brow, If ever I loved Thee, my Jesus, 'tis now." My mom's appearance had changed in those final days. Fragile and tiny, she was now wearing a child-sized diaper, her eye sockets were sunk in, her coloring turned gray, her hands were colder than usual, and her toes and feet turned black. Her breathing, even with the oxygen machine to help her, was labored. A terrifying rattling and gurgling sound filled the air around us as we waited in her room. I had a new definition of the death dew lying cold on one's brow. Yet I know my mom's resounding song in those final days was "If ever I loved Thee, my Jesus, 'tis now." Her confidence and love for Jesus never wavered. Our family begged Jesus to take her home, to bring an end to the horror and suffering she was experiencing.

After days of being awake and holding watch by her bed, the moment happened as I had pictured it. My dad was at her head, holding her and whispering to her that it was okay; my brother, sister-in-law and I were gathered at her side. Sobs shook the room. In her final moments at 7:25 a.m. on Friday April 1, 2016, my mom lifted her hand as if she were either saying good-bye to us or waving hello to someone in the next life. I whispered to her, "I'll be there soon, Mom."

I stood there on what seemed like the edge of eternity, and my mom passed from our arms here on Earth into the arms of Jesus. Her labored, rattling breathing stopped in a beautiful, peaceful glimpse of the sweetness of Heaven. I knew she had been given a new body and new breath in her lungs. I hit the off button on her oxygen machine, and all was strangely silent. A mix of overpowering, indescribable grief, utter exhaustion, and a sweet relief for my mom covered me.

2 Timothy 4:7 came to my mind: "I have fought the good fight, I have finished the race, I have kept the faith." My mom had finished the race. She was free now—no longer suffering, no longer struggling, no longer lying in a body ridden with cancer.

A year earlier, on April 1, 2015, as mentioned earlier in this book, my journal entry held these words: "But if not…you are still good—still Lord, still King!" I believed those words. I believed them as we let go of my mom and watched her pass from this world into the arms of Jesus. I believed them as the funeral home men rolled my mother's body on a stretcher out of our home for the last time. The grief was overwhelming as I stood outside watching them put her body in the hearse. I sobbed loudly, wondering if the neighbors might learn of my mom's death through hearing my shrieking cries carried in the breeze that morning. Yet though I grieved, I believed that God was still good, still Lord, and still King!

12

THE FOG

PEOPLE HAD TOLD me about the fog that often comes down after a major loss like this one. It's true. For me, the fog started with a supernatural grace from the Lord. He carried me through the next few days as we picked out a casket and flowers and made a myriad of other choices for the funeral. It's as though I were watching someone else go through the motions. There were so many details to think through and so many people coming to town (we have an incredibly large family). My task-oriented hostess personality kicked into gear, and I had little time to think about the reason for the gathering. The fog continued through the day of the funeral—the Lord gave me strength I didn't know I had to make it through the day.

Then the funeral was over. Our gigantic family all went back to their respective homes. Our house—which for months had been Grand Central Station with friends, family, nurses, and neighbors in and out—was suddenly quiet. My dad and I no longer carried the identity of "caregiver," and we weren't sure what to do with ourselves.

A week later, I returned to Raleigh to resume a life that hadn't been normal for seventeen months. I didn't know where to start. My heart broken and my identity shaken, I was now motherless, no longer a care-giver, and having a hard time knowing how to function. While things were spinning quickly in the typical fast-paced American frenzy, I was moving in slow motion.

On April 11th, I wrote the following in my journal:

Today marks one week since I buried my mother—such a strange mix of overpowering grief and exhaling relief. Simultaneously heartbroken and hopeful, I know that my mom no longer faces cancer, pain, discharge, weakness, loneliness, etc. I know that she stands strong in the presence of a good, good Father. And I know that she walks on streets of gold, worships with the veil lifted, sees in whole what I only see in part. She is doing great. She got what was best. She wins. But oh, the grief for us who are left behind! It causes me at times to catch my breath, this emo-tional pain that causes you to stop breathing as physical pain can do. I must at times remind myself to breathe.

And now I am back in Raleigh, and life must go on. How might I honor Mom and her life so well lived as I finish out my days here on Earth? How can I go on in the midst of this breathtak-ing grief? It seems the world and all the people in it continue on around me in a frenzy. I feel like I am in slow motion, coming out of a fog, reteaching myself to walk, breathe, live, etc.

So for today, Lord, give me strength to make it through a day, grace to let go of the things that may not get done and freedom to rest in the process.

Days continued in this fog. Sometimes I walked in denial, pretending that my mom was just fine and that I would see her the next time I made it to Goldsboro. But soon I would snap out of that reality when I would go to call her or text her to tell her about something that happened in my day. Most days, by the grace of God, I was in this fog because the numbness was safe for the moment. The weight of the grief, were I to fully bear it, would have been too heavy.

Days turned into weeks, and the fog began to lift ever so slightly. Deep waves of grief would find their way in, reminding me that my worst nightmare had in fact come true. But when I could not stand under the pressure of the grief any longer, the fog would cover me again, a sanctuary from reality. At times, I invited the grief to draw me out of the fog, instigating the sobs with trips into my mom's closet, where I could wrap myself in her robe and smell her scent. There were times when I deliberately listened to her voice in old voicemails and read her words in old text messages.

On April 24th, I wrote the following in my journal:

At times the grief feels suffocating, oppressive, as if someone is holding my head under water and I am fighting for air just to catch my next breath. At other times, I am going through the motions of any day, and one looking on would barely know the hell I have been through recently.

This cycle of pressing into the grief and then retreating into the fog continued through the summer months. Almost four months after my mom's death, I attended our thirty-seventh annual family beach trip, with over fifty cousins in and out during that week. A sorrow hung over the week, as we all desperately missed my mom being there. On the first evening of the trip, we all went out on the beach, the youngest generation splashing in the waves and the older generations standing around as the sun set, sharing and catching up since we were last together. That evening, the largest rainbow I have ever seen stretched itself out across the water and toward the pier. It was as if my mom was smiling down and God was sending a reminder of His goodness and promises to us. In that moment, admiring the rainbow, I felt the fog was lifting and I was beginning to feel more and more like myself. I was no longer just going through the motions, numb, and in slow motion. Instead, I felt somewhat back to normal. The following Saturday morning, as our week together came to a close, another rainbow appeared out over the water. It was the perfect closure to a healing week.

I would still give all that I have for one more conversation with my mom, one more hug, or one more chance to hear her voice, to look into her eyes, and to have her look into mine. She could always see straight through to my heart. The constant ache of her absence still follows me daily. A piece of me will always be missing. Every day, an unexpected lump will form in my throat, and the tears will surface as I come to grips again with my new reality. They say the greater the love, the greater the loss. My loss is great, and so I choose to be grateful for the gift God gave me in the great love I received from my mother and friend. I don't take the special relationship we had for granted. What we had was special and not a guarantee in all mother-daughter relationships. I know I will always live with a layer of pain and sadness in my life, even during times of great joy and laughter, because my mom will be missing.

As I searched for gratitude in the midst of the deep pain of grief those months following my mom's death, I realized that intimacy with the Lord looked different on the other side of this horrific event. I am different today than I was when everything in life seemed to be good. And knowing God *is* different when you can run His character through the filter of an unraveling life. There is an intimacy to experiencing the presence of God in the midst of hell on earth that is different than what I had experienced when life seemed, for the most part, to be going well. For that, I can be grateful, even in the midst of the fog when it seemed I didn't even have the energy to thank Him.

13

ETERNAL LIFE

IN THE BEST book on grief and loss I have found, *A Grace Disguised*, Jerry Sittser describes loss like this:

> Though entirely unique (as all losses are), it is a manifestation of a universal experience. Sooner or later all people suffer loss, in little doses or big ones, suddenly or over time, privately or in public settings. Loss is as much a part of normal life as birth, for as surely as we are born into this world, we suffer loss before we leave it.

> It is not, therefore, the experience of loss that becomes the defining moment of our lives, for that is as inevitable as death, which is the last loss awaiting us all. It is how we *respond* to loss that matters. That response will largely determine the quality, the direction, and the impact of our lives.

As a believer and follower of Jesus, and because my mom was as well, I view this horrible loss in my life and hers through the lens of eternity.

I believe that for anyone who has life in Christ, death is not an ending, but is instead a beginning—a beginning that we would all welcome and long for if we truly grasped its reality. Does this change the grief and loss that I feel on this side of eternity? By no means. The loss is still very real. The deep ache in my heart is present every single day, as I miss my mom. But does this change the hope that I have in the wake of her loss? Absolutely. I know where my mom is and I know that I will join her one day soon—for that I cannot wait! John 3:16 says, "For God so loved the world, that He gave his only Son, that whoever believes in Him should not perish but have eternal life." Because of my mom's faith, I can be sure that she has eternal life with God in Heaven.

There is a popular country song right now by Cole Swindell called, "You Should Be Here." I heard it for the first time about two months after my mom died while I was on a seven-hour road trip to Maryland for a time set aside to specifically process and grieve her death. The song played multiple times on the radio during that trip. It speaks of wishing that a loved one could still be here for all of life's moments. Every time I hear this song, I cry. I cry for the moments that my mom is missing: the birthdays, the dance recitals of her grandchildren, the beautiful sunsets or the crisp colors in the flowerbeds, and the future graduations and weddings that she will not be here to attend. I cry because the pain of missing her is raw and real, and I just wish that she were back here on this earth doing all of the things that she did before she got sick.

But the more I think about it, the more I realize that it would be cruel and unfair for her to be back here now. After tasting Heaven and all that it entails (things that my mind can't begin to fathom), it would be cruel for her to be placed back in this place called Earth. I can sing this song and wish for her to be here, sure. If I truly understood the reality of eternity, I would not wish for her return. She faced death once—a horrific, long-suffering death. I would never want her to go through that again. Knowing what she knows now and having seen and experienced what she has experienced, she wouldn't want to be here again. When I hear this song, I cry because I miss my mom, but I also smile, because she is so much better off than she ever could have been or ever would have been staying here on Earth. I don't know exactly how Heaven works, but I pray that there are times that God gives my mom a window down to see the birthdays, the dance recitals, and other moments of our family's joy.

In Paul's letter to the Philippians, he writes about faith in Christ:

But whatever gain I had, I counted as loss for the sake of Christ. Indeed, I count everything as loss because of the surpassing worth of knowing Christ Jesus my Lord. For His sake I have suffered the loss of all things and count them as rubbish, in order that I may gain Christ and be found in Him, not having a righteousness of my own that comes from the law, but that which comes through faith in Christ, the righteousness from God that depends on faith—that I may know Him and the power of His resurrection, and may share His sufferings, becoming like Him in His death, that by any means possible I may attain the resurrection from the dead. (Phil. 3:7–11)

My mother had joy as she shared in Christ's sufferings. She had joy as she experienced great loss—the loss of her freedom, her ability to do things, her dignity, and ultimately, her life. She was once an incredibly capable woman who managed and ran things with ease and excellence. As that was stripped away, she retained her joy because it was all rubbish compared to the joy of knowing Christ Jesus her Lord.

My mom's salvation and key to Heaven was not as a result of her goodness or righteousness, though many would say that she was perhaps one of the most righteous they had met. You would be hard pressed to find anyone who would say anything negative about her. However, that doesn't matter when our time here on Earth comes to an end. We are all sinners who fall short of the glory of God, no matter how good we may seem here on Earth. My mom's salvation and her key to Heaven came strictly from Christ's righteousness and her faith in Him, not on anything she did during her lifetime.

2 Corinthians 5:21 says, "For our sake He made Him to be sin who knew no sin, so that in Him we might become the righteousness of God." Because of Jesus's perfect, sinless life and His death on the cross that bore the weight of our sin, we can now have eternal life with God through Christ. When God looks at those of us who believe, He sees the righteousness of Christ, and our sin has been completely washed away. Such good news! Because my mom knew Jesus and had a personal relationship with Him, and because of Christ taking her place on the cross, she did not have to experience eternal separation from God but instead now stands in His presence and is truly Home.

Philippians 3:20–21 says, "But our citizenship is in heaven, and from it we await a Savior, the Lord Jesus Christ, who will transform our lowly body to be like His glorious body, by the power that enables Him even to subject all things to Himself." Our citizenship is in Heaven. We were made to live in God's presence. Every heart here on Earth longs for the place it was made for, for the Home where all will be as it was meant to be. C.S. Lewis said, "If I find in myself desires which nothing in this world can satisfy, the only logical explanation is that I was made for another world." The longings of my mother's heart have been fulfilled. She now is at rest and peace in the place that her heart was made for, face to face with the God, whom she loves and for whom she was created.

My current reality (and yours, if you are reading this) is that we still live in the middle of the story. Eternity still awaits us on the other side of this life. It is still the "not yet" of our stories. For those who believe in Jesus, our "not yet" will one day be fulfilled, and with that, I can whisper with confidence in the air to my mom, "I'm coming soon." My heart longs for that day when I will join her and Jesus in the place that my heart longs for.

Almost a year before my mom's death, after her cancer-free report, I wrote the following verse and subsequent thoughts in my journal:

So when God desired to show more convincingly to the heirs of the promise the unchangeable character of His purpose, He guaranteed it with an oath, so that by two unchangeable things, in which it is impossible for God to lie, we who have fled for refuge might have strong encouragement to *hold fast* to the hope set before us. We have this as a sure and steadfast anchor of the soul, a hope that enters into the inner peace behind the curtain, where Jesus has gone as a forerunner on our behalf. (Heb. 6:17–20)

Jesus, thank you for going as a forerunner on my behalf behind the curtain. Thank you for sacrificing it all so that the veil might be torn and a sinner like me might have access to the King. Jesus, thank you for ultimate *hope* that you secured—the anchor for my soul—that the things I hope for in this life are not ultimate or final, but hoping for eternity **is secure, is ultimate,** and **will be fulfilled!** Lord Jesus, thank you for the small glimpse of hope fulfilled with removing mom's cancer. Lord, if it is your will, would you continue to give me glimpses of hope fulfilled on this side of eternity, as I ultimately hope for and long for that.

I now read this journal entry knowing that it was not God's will for my mom to continue to live on this earth. My dream of having more time with my mom is over. My dream of hearing her voice longer, feeling her touch longer, and enjoying her presence longer is gone. But ultimately, true hope is still fulfilled because I know where my mom is and because I know time here is temporary. One day soon, I will be with her (and more importantly, Jesus!) again. I prayed diligently for God to remove her cancer and to heal her body. Though not how I expected, He did answer that prayer to the fullest—her body has been healed and restored, forever.

At my mom's funeral, my family had our pastor read the following letter from us:

Dear Friends and Family,

First of all, we want to thank you for your love and care for Lynda and our family over the last seventeen months. Thank you for the cards, the calls, the texts, the meals, the flowers, and the visits to show you care. And thank you so much for being here today to remember and help us celebrate the life of the most selfless and sacrificial woman we have ever met. We are grateful for each of you who are here.

Second, and most importantly, we want you to know that while we are experiencing devastating heartbreak today, we do not grieve without hope. Many might say that cancer has won. And yes, cancer has shortened Lynda's life here on Earth. But we would say that cancer did not win.

Because Lynda had a personal relationship with Jesus and believed in His paying the penalty for her sins, we know with certainty that on Friday when she breathed her last breath here on Earth, she immediately stood in His presence and was ushered into a better life—a life with no more pain, no more tears, no more crying, and no more cancer. Life didn't end for Lynda on Friday; instead, it really began that day. And for those who also believe in Jesus, we will get to join her someday soon. Life here on Earth is just a vapor, just a small point on an eternal line. She got to begin the best part of her life—the eternal part in the arms of Jesus—sooner than we expected. In this case, she really got what was best.

There was an anonymous poem posted on the wall in the chemo room at UNC that Lynda loved to read. It says:

WHAT CANCER CANNOT DO!
Cancer is so limited.
It cannot cripple love,
It cannot shatter hope,
It cannot corrode faith,
It cannot destroy peace,
It cannot kill friendship,
It cannot suppress memories,
It cannot silence courage,
It cannot invade the soul,
It cannot steal eternal life,
It cannot conquer the spirit.

And we want to add a line: Cancer cannot separate you from the love of God. And that is how we have gotten through this. Cancer does not win. Death does not win. And for that reason, we can truly say, "It is well."

Bruce, Bert, Allison, and Cam

Seventeen months before my mom's death, I reread every journal I had ever written and was reminded of God's character:

Kind	Rock	Friend	God who hears
Faithful	Truth	Satisfier	God who understands
Holy	Gracious	King	Pursuer
Pure	Merciful	Lamb	Sanctifier
Just	Patient	Lion	Healer
Jealous	Good	Shepherd	Great Physician
Warrior	Beginning/End	Redeemer	Great I Am
Protector	Near	Lover of my soul	Most beautiful
Provider	Sympathizes	Comforter	Most valuable
Sovereign	Caring	True joy	All-Present
In control	Careful	Trustworthy	All-Powerful
Worthy	Savior	Praiseworthy	All-Knowing
Constant	Father	Strong	Binds up wounds of the brokenhearted
Only True God	Maker	God who saves	Love
Defender	Creator	God who sees	Brings beauty from ashes

The truths of the list I made in my journal that day continue to point me to the One who is the anchor for my soul. He is the only One trustworthy in the storms of this life. He is the only One worthy for which to hold fast.

"I have fought the good fight, I have finished the race, I have kept the faith" (2 Tim. 4:7).
Lynda P. Malpass
April 17, 1953 – April 1, 2016

Mom and me in the chemo infusion room, February 2015

Mom ringing the "I finished chemo" bell at UNC, April 2015

Family photoshoot, November 2015

Family photoshoot, November 2015

Family photoshoot, November 2015

Family photoshoot, November 2015

47798689R00059

Made in the USA
Middletown, DE
02 September 2017